THE ONLY Memory Improvement BOOK YOU'LL EVER NEED

THE BRAIN GAMES, PUZZLES, AND KNOW-HOW YOU NEED TO KEEP YOUR MIND SHARP

Puzzles by Charles Timmerman, Founder of Funster.com
Edited by Rudolph C. Hatfield, PhD

Aadamsmedia
Avon, Massachusetts

Published by
Adams Media, a division of F+W Media, Inc.
57 Littlefield Street, Avon, MA 02322. U.S.A.
www.adamsmedia.com

Contains material adapted and abridged from *The Everything® More Memory Booster Puzzles Book* by Charles Timmerman, copyright © 2010 by F+W Media, Inc., ISBN: 10 1-4405-0555-1, ISBN 13: 978-1-4405-0555-3; *The Everything® Memory Booster Puzzles Book* by Charles Timmerman, copyright © 2008 by F+W Media, Inc., ISBN 10: 1-59869-383-2, ISBN 13: 978-1-59869-383-6; *The Everything® Crossword & Puzzle Book, Volume II* by Charles Timmerman, copyright © 2009 by F+W Media, Inc., ISBN 10: 1-60550-047-X, ISBN 13: 978-1-60550-047-8; *The Everything® 15-Minute Sudoku Book* by Charles Timmerman, copyright © 2006 by F+W Media, Inc., ISBN 10: 1-59869-054-X, ISBN 13: 978-1-59869-054-5; *365 Ways to Boost Your Brain Power* by Carolyn Dean, MD, Valentine Dmitriev, PhD, and Donna Raskin, copyright © 2009 by F+W Media, Inc., ISBN 10: 1-60550-060-7, ISBN 13: 978-1-60550-060-7.

ISBN 10: 1-4405-6564-3
ISBN 13: 978-1-4405-6564-9

Printed in the United States of America.

10 9 8 7 6 5 4 3 2 1

This book is available at quantity discounts for bulk purchases.
For information, please call 1-800-289-0963.

CONTENTS

INTRODUCTION

Everyone knows that physical exercise can keep our bodies healthy—just ask any of the millions of people who regularly visit a gym. However, new research tells us that we can also keep our brains fit with regular mental exercise. That's what this book is all about: mental aerobics that can give your memory and brain functionality a boost.

Why do we need to keep our brains mentally fit? Well, some people just want to confidently connect names to faces in social situations. Others want to reduce their number of "senior moments," a euphemism for episodes of forgetfulness, which can happen at any age. For all of us, mental agility is increasingly important to be successful in the world today. In this information age, we need sharp brains to keep us afloat in a flood of data. The good news is that scientific research suggests that memory improvement games can stimulate our brains and foster mental agility. This book won't teach you how to juggle, but it will present you with numerous brain-building challenges in the form of fun and engaging puzzles as well as helpful lifestyle tips for keeping your brain healthy.

In a study published in the *New England Journal of Medicine*, researchers found that people could reduce their risk of Alzheimer's disease by adding one mentally stimulating activity per week. Adding more activities, such as working a crossword puzzle every day, was even better. Research also points to lifestyle changes that can give your brain a boost. A healthy low-fat diet with lots of fruits and vegetables is important to keeping your brain in peak condition. Staying physically fit benefits the brain as well as the rest of the body. And reducing stress will cut down on the mental wear and tear that keeps your mind from working efficiently. Doing all of these things—in addition to the mental aerobics in this book—can help give your memory a boost.

Motivation is important, so have fun as you start your training with these puzzles. Hopefully, you will look forward to the challenges. There is a diversity of puzzles in this book, and some you will enjoy more than others. Give them all a chance—the ones that are the most frustrating at the start might become the most satisfying once they are mastered. It is okay to pick and choose from your favorites, but be sure to cross-train with a variety of puzzles for the most effective brain work-out. Your memory will work best if you have a positive, confident attitude. You can remember if you think you can!

How to Use This Book

While the puzzles here vary from easy to difficult, they were all created to engage your brain, not melt it down. Start at Memory Level 1 and work your way through each puzzle in the chapter. It may take you some time to figure out the answers, and you may not even be able to solve them all, but remember, you're just starting out. As you progress through each of the fifteen chapters, you may find yourself recalling answers much more quickly and perhaps even finding that your memory has improved in your day-to-day life. For an added challenge, this book includes space for you to record how long it takes you to complete the puzzles in each chapter, so that you can better track your results over time.

Types of Puzzles

Working on puzzles, such as the daily crossword puzzle, sudoku puzzle, or word scrambles, will help stimulate your brain. They provide an easy way to strengthen and maintain several different areas of cognitive function, including memory and visual-spatial areas. This book includes a variety of puzzles that will help keep your brain fit without ever causing it extra stress.

Forget Me Not

Forget Me Not puzzles present a simple challenge: Remember lists of random items. This might sound difficult at first, but it will become easy and fun when you use the link system. It will help you create a memorable image for each neighboring pair. You'll vividly see each image in your mind's eye.

The Link System

The idea behind the link system is to make a mental chain out of the list of items to be remembered. This is done by associating each item in the list with the next item in some memorable way. For example, if you want to remember the list "tree," "wheel," "knee," "house," "hat," and "ferry," you would first start out by thinking of a mental image to associate "tree" with "wheel." This could be done by imagining a wheel sitting next to a tree—a logical choice, but not really a memorable one. Let your imagination go wild and try to think of things that you would surely remember if you saw them in the real world. Actually "see" one of these images in your mind's eye. Now when you think of the word "tree," you should think of the word "wheel." For a link to work best, the items should interact with each other. Don't just imagine the two items sitting next to each other; they should actually do something with each other. Also, include lots of detail in your images to help lock the mental pictures into your memory.

As a check, immediately see if you can remember each item by running through all the links without looking. Then later in the day, or perhaps the next day, try to remember each item without looking at the list. You should even be able to run through a Forget Me Not list backwards by using the links in reverse.

You will probably get faster at memorizing the lists as you get more experienced associating word pairs. This is a good thing, and it shows that your mind is more able to focus.

Crosswords

The crossword puzzles in this book are similar to the kind you'd find while reading the *New York Times*, only easier. You will need to use the clues provided to complete the puzzle, which consists of a grid of squares and blanks. Each word will be written out either vertically or horizontally on the grid. It's okay if you can't fill in every entry; you will still be getting a good mental workout.

Word Searches

All of the word search puzzles in this book are in the traditional format. Words are hidden in a grid of letters in any direction: horizontal, vertical, diagonal, forward, or backward. Words can also overlap. For example, the letters at the end of the word "mast" could be used as the start of the word "stern." Only the letters A–Z are used, and any spaces in an entry are removed. For example, "tropical fish" would be found in the grid as "tropicalfish."

Sudoku

Sudoku is played on a 9 × 9 grid. Heavier lines subdivide this grid into nine 3 × 3 boxes. The object is to fill in the grid so that every row, column, and 3 × 3 box contains the numbers one through nine with no repeats. The puzzle begins with some of the numbers already entered. There will always be only one solution for each puzzle.

Providers

Provider puzzles are similar to sudoku puzzles in the sense that you must fill the grid so that every row and column fits together. The list of words you can use is categorized by how many letters each word has: three, four, five, or more letters. You must fit all of the words into the grids. To get you started, one of the words is already entered.

Cryptoquotes

With Cryptoquote puzzles, you'll have to figure out which letter of the alphabet (A–Z) has been substituted with another letter. Your challenge is to break the code for each puzzle and decipher the quote and author. If you get stumped, you can refer to the hints below the puzzle to help guide you toward the answer.

Double Scrambles

The object of Double Scramble puzzles is to unscramble the letters to form words. However, the challenge doesn't end there: You'll also need to unscramble the first letters of the words you made to form a word related to the title. Keep in mind that some groups of letters can be unscrambled in more than one way. For example, the letters ASEHC can be rearranged to form CHASE or ACHES. In these cases, part of the fun is to determine the correct words so that the final answer can be formed using the first letters from each word.

CHAPTER 1

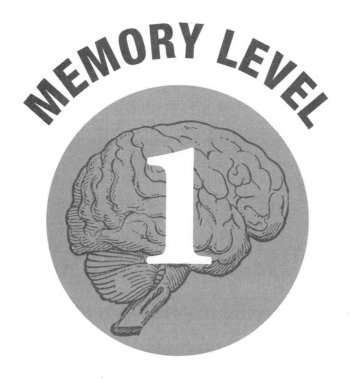

MEMORY LEVEL
1

Puzzle 1.01
Forget Me Not

chest	cushion
egg	cord
scissors	bucket
screw	roof
table	lock

Puzzle 1.01
Forget Me Not

_____   _____

_____   _____

_____   _____

_____   _____

_____   _____

Puzzle 1.02
Provider

3 LETTERS

BEE
CUE
EAU
ERA
ESS
HAE
HOE

OAR
PAS
REP
ROC
SEE
SHH
TAO

4 LETTERS

ALAS
ALEE
ALES
ALTS
ANAS
ANTE
ARES
ARIA
BARB
COOL
COTE
DAPS
ERNE
EROS
GOLD
IRIS
LASE
LIRE

LOAN
LOOS
MAYO
NOTA
ORAD
ORLE
PART
PERT
REST
ROSE
RUSE
SLOE
STAR
TARP
TATE
TEAS
TOYS
URGE

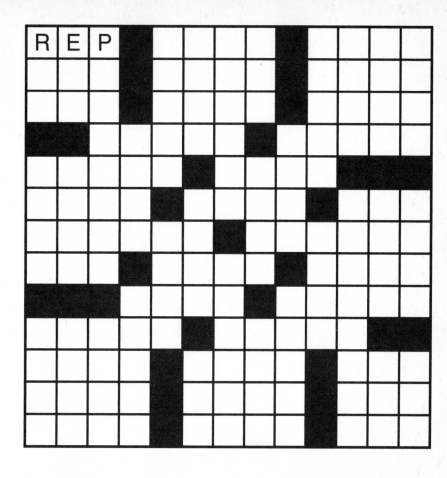

5 LETTERS

ACMES
AROSE
BALLS
CATER
CEDES

COSTS
GATES
RIALS
SALSA
TENSE

8 LETTERS

PRESAGES
PROTESTS

6 LETTERS

LEARNT
NEARER

RESALE
SIESTA

Puzzle 1.03
Cryptoquote

YT VNS STG, ES EYXX QSCSCZSQ TIV VNS EIQGO

IB IHQ STSCYSO, ZHV VNS OYXSTPS IB IHQ

BQYSTGO.

—CRQVYT XHVNSQ JYTW FQ.

Hint: The word "silence" is found in the quote.

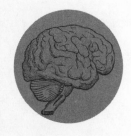

Think Holistically

We have ample evidence to support the notion that psychological health affects physical health, and vice versa. It's vital to your overall health and your brain's health to think holistically—to view yourself as a whole being, not simply a collection of parts. In the 1970s, when Buddhist ideas seeped into Western culture, one essential message was: "I am not my liver, my spleen, my blood, nor my brain. I am all of me." It sounded new and often revolutionary at the time, but science soon joined the chorus. You are not the sum of all your parts; you are the sum of all your parts operating in tandem. Mind, body, and spirit are inseparable, and illness in one may leave us vulnerable to illness in other areas. Think holistically and your overall health, as well as your brain's health, can improve.

Puzzle 1.04
Crossword

Across

1. Prefix with red or structure
4. ___-Wan Kenobi
7. Clinton's attorney general
8. Reject
10. Poison
11. Washington bills
12. Public spat
13. Map within a map
17. Past pudgy
18. Former spouses
20. Light bulb unit
22. Coral formation
24. "A mouse!"
26. Roll call response
29. 500 sheets
31. Bert's Muppet pal
32. Doctors' org.
33. Wound up
35. Actress Zellweger
37. ___-garde
38. Nike's swoosh, e.g.
39. Ocean motion
41. Narcissist's love
42. Get-up-and-go

Down

2. Supermodel Campbell
3. Golfer Palmer, informally
4. Lennon's love
5. ___ fide
6. Crude cartel
9. Where the deer and the antelope play
14. Place to build
15. Chewy candy
16. Wish granter
18. Raring to go
19. Total
20. Part of WWW
21. Have a go at
23. Spooky
25. Actress Winslet
27. Christopher of "Superman"
28. Panoramic view
30. Track event
32. Book of maps
34. Down in the dumps
35. It's over your head
36. Billionth: Prefix
40. "___ had it up to here!"

Puzzle 1.05
Sudoku

8			7	1	5			4
		5	3		6	7		
3		6	4		8	9		1
	6			5			4	
			8		7			
	5			4			9	
6		9	5		3	4		2
		4	9		2	5		
5			1	6	4			9

Puzzle 1.06
Sudoku

3	4		8	2	6		7	1
		8				9		
7	6			9			4	3
	8		1		2		3	
	3						9	
	7		9		4		1	
8	2			4			5	9
		7				3		
4	1		3	8	9		6	2

Puzzle 1.07
Word Search

AL PACINO
AMY IRVING
ANDY GARCIA
ANNE BAXTER
BETTE MIDLER
BETTY GRABLE
CARY GRANT
CHER
CLARK GABLE
DEMI MOORE
ELLEN BURSTYN
ERROL FLYNN
FAYE DUNAWAY
GARY BUSEY
GENE AUTRY
GLENN CLOSE
HARPO MARX
HEDY LAMARR
HENRY FONDA
JAMES CAAN
JAMES DEAN
JANE WYMAN
JOAN CRAWFORD
JOHN CANDY
JOHNNY DEPP
JULIE ANDREWS
LANA TURNER
LIZA MINELLI
MAE WEST
MEG RYAN
MEL GIBSON
MERYL STREEP

PETER FALK
PETER FONDA
RAQUEL WELCH
RED BUTTONS
RIP TORN
TOM HANKS
VIVIEN LEIGH
YUL BRYNNER

```
O N I C A P L A Y D N A C N H O J C M M
C E S O L C N N E L G H C X Y D G Y W E
A N P U A X A M Y I R V I N G C A U W G
J I R E L D I M E T T E B N H W R L K R
A L M O E A N W E T S E W E A M Y B A Y
M S E A T R N O S B I R R N J V B R N A
E H P R N P T A F W L Z U C O I U Y N N
S E A E O D I S T R E D Y B A V S N E P
D D L D T O Y R L U E R M J N I E N B P
E Y B B N E M G B Y R T D G C E Y E A E
A L G U A O R I A E R N E N R N L R X D
N A E T A G F F M R T E E P A L N L T Y
A M N T A E K Y A E C T M R W E K X E N
M A E O V K C R R L D I Y R F I I C R N
Y R A N T O M H A N K S A G O G H L Y H
W R U S H C L E W L E U Q A R H P J U O
E X T N A R G Y R A C H M Y D A A D Q J
N X R A M O P R A H F M E L G I B S O N
A S Y E J R Y C L I Z A M I N E L L I Q
J J A M E S C A A N Y L F L O R R E Y
```

Puzzle 1.08
Double Scramble

Lighter Alternative

IILCV   _____

WLOTE   _____

ELHTO   _____

ERYCM   _____

AONNY   _____

_____

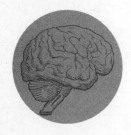

Snack Smartly

Choosing snacks wisely can help fuel your body between meals, give you an energy boost, and add to your total intake of essential nutrients for the day, which will keep your brain—and body—healthy as you age. Snacking can also help take the edge off hunger between meals. The key to smart snacking is the type and amounts of food that you choose. Here are some things to consider when snacking:

- Choose snacks that are lower in fat and nutrient-rich.
- Plan and eat snacks well ahead of mealtime.
- Make snacks part of your eating plan for the day instead of thinking of them as an extra.
- Make snacking a conscious activity.
- Eat smaller-portioned snacks, not meal-sized ones.

Puzzle 1.09
Provider

3 LETTERS

AGE
ALA
ARE
ASS
CON
DIG
DUO
EON
HAP
HOT
NET
NIP
ORA

OXY
PAL
RIA
SAE
SAT
SEA
SOS
SPA
SRI
TAR
TEE
TOR

4 LETTERS

ADOS
ANES
ANNA
APED
APES
APOD
ASEA
BEET
CEES
CODA
KALE
LANE
LOOP
LOSE
LUXE

OAKS
OATS
ONES
ORES
PAGE
PALS
PHAT
PSST
SAPS
SARI
SASS
SECS
SEED
SEEP
SELL

SETT
SHAD
SLAG
SOLO

SORE
SOYS
SPAS
SPAT

5 LETTERS

ASSET
ENDED
ESSES
ESTER

SLATS
STABS
TAILS

Puzzle 1.10
Cryptoquote

RAGV GZKLDWMQVM SWIV. SA RAGVFM, Z IAIVKS

JZK CV VSVFKWSO, VSVFKWSO JZK CV SQV SWJE

AY Z JRAJE.

—IZFO XZFFWMQ

Hint: The word "clock" is found in the quote.

Puzzle 1.11
Cryptoquote

LXLOKPUL GH D WLUGQH DI ALDHI PUEL D

KLDO. D OLDA WLUGQH BDH BGH POGWGUDA

GFLDH EAPHLO IPWLIBLO.

—WLPOW E. AGEBILURLOW

Hint: The word "original" is found in the quote.

Puzzle 1.12
Crossword

Across

1. Japanese wrestling
3. Singleton
5. Rarer than rare
7. Pied Piper follower
8. Picture puzzle
9. Kind of lily
12. Custard dessert
13. Abduct
16. Actor Neeson
19. Artist Matisse
20. Turn away
21. Balloon filler
23. Bar bill
24. Proposer's prop
25. Marathoner's staying power
28. Short snooze
30. Bother
31. Bangkok native
33. Put in stitches
36. Fashionably nostalgic
37. "Big" London landmark
38. Mad Hatter's drink
39. Chip dip
40. Supreme Diana
41. Pancake topper

Down

1. T-bone, e.g.
2. Director Welles
3. Hooter
4. Mayberry's town drunk
6. Jazzy Fitzgerald
7. Sought office
10. In flames
11. "Raging Bull" subject
14. Thickheaded
15. Assumed name
17. Nose-in-the-air type
18. ___ Lee cakes
19. Clue
22. ___-bitsy
26. ___ Dame
27. "___ takers?"
28. ___ King Cole
29. Buenos ___
30. Wonderment
32. Get wind of
34. Online auctioneer
35. "2001" computer
38. Tic-___-toe

Puzzle 1.13
Sudoku

9	2		4		6		7	1
			9	3	7			
7				1				5
1	7		8		5		4	6
			1		2			
4	9		7		3		2	8
5				2				7
			6	8	1			
3	1		5		9		8	4

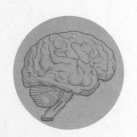

Exercise 30 Minutes a Day

Regular exercise—at least 20 minutes a day, but 30 minutes to an hour daily is best—is one great way to preserve your mental acuity. Aerobic exercise helps get the blood coursing through your system, carrying oxygen and glucose—two substances the brain needs in order to function—to your brain. Regular exercise also can create healthier connections in the brain. Though studies are still underway to establish the link between exercise and increased brain neurons, many researchers—including those involved with Alzheimer's disease research—are studying the protective effects of regular physical exercise on the brain's neural paths for transmitting signals.

Puzzle 1.14
Double Scramble

Salad Dressing Choice

HDAER   _____

LOOCR   _____

IDARO   _____

EREVN   _____

ULADT   _____

_____

Puzzle 1.15
Double Scramble

Supersized

EONJY   _____

EKLNA   _____

YALOL   _____

ELDIG   _____

ERACH   _____

_____

Puzzle 1.16
Sudoku

```
8 . . | . 6 . | 5 . 3
5 . 1 | 3 . . | . . .
. . 2 | . 8 . | . 1 .
------+-------+------
6 . 3 | 8 . . | . . .
1 . 9 | 7 . 6 | 4 . 2
. . . | . . 1 | 6 . 7
------+-------+------
. 1 . | . 5 . | 8 . .
. . . | . . 8 | 3 . 9
3 . 8 | . 4 . | . . 5
```

Puzzle 1.17
Sudoku

```
3 . . | 9 . 6 | . . 1
2 . . | . . . | . . 4
. 6 . | 4 . 2 | . 9 .
------+-------+------
8 1 2 | . . . | 3 5 6
. . . | . . . | . . .
9 5 7 | . . . | 4 1 8
------+-------+------
. 8 . | 3 . 7 | . 6 .
5 . . | . . . | . . 2
7 . . | 5 . 1 | . . 9
```

Puzzle 1.18
Forget Me Not

plane	kettle
friend	bottle
hole	train
brush	umbrella
library	hat

Puzzle 1.18
Forget Me Not

_____   _____

_____   _____

_____   _____

_____   _____

_____   _____

What Was Your Time?

If you decided to challenge yourself further and time your puzzling session, be sure to write down your results below. Take a moment to reflect on your past sessions and acknowledge any improvements made along the way. With every chapter in this book, you should be able to notice how much more focused and alert your brain is becoming.

_____

_____

_____

_____

_____

_____

_____

_____

_____

_____

_____

_____

_____

_____

_____

CHAPTER 2

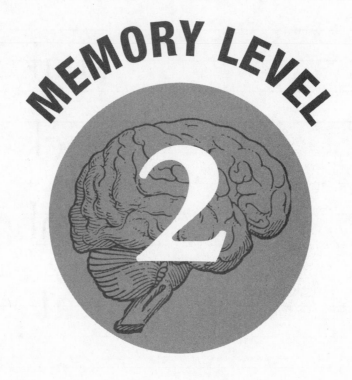

MEMORY LEVEL

2

hospital	jewel
army	snake
stomach	sock
fly	umbrella
floor	leaf

Puzzle 2.01
Forget Me Not

_____   _____

_____   _____

_____   _____

_____   _____

_____   _____

Puzzle 2.02
Provider

3 LETTERS

AHA	LOP
ALP	MIX
ANE	MOA
ARC	OLE
ARM	PEA
ART	POD
ASP	PUG
AXE	RIB
DIN	SAL
LET	SHE
LIE	SOT
LOO	

4 LETTERS

ALLS	POLO
AMPS	RIMS
ANTA	RIOT
AREA	ROOT
ARIL	ROUT
ARTS	SADE
ASPS	SCAT
CEPE	SEAL
CORE	SHEA
DEMO	SHIN
EAST	SLAT
EELS	SLOT
LAMA	TAGS
LONE	TALL
MODE	TEAT
OLIO	TELE
PENT	TODS

5 LETTERS

ALIAS	STETS
ASSES	TESTA
ESTOP	TESTS
PORTS	TSARS
ROBLE	

6 LETTERS

LESSEE	SPARSE

Puzzle 2.03
Cryptoquote

UDDYRLAF XIGF HYNH: U XIGF NI L JFPYLHF

U TFFS NIL. DYRLAF XIGF HYNH: U TFFS NIL

JFPYLHF U XIGF NIL.

—FAUPM KAIDD

Hint: The word "mature" is found in the quote.

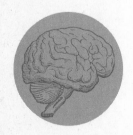

Detoxify Your Brain

To cleanse your body of common toxins, such as pollutants or household chemicals, you can try the following: flaxseed, licorice root, ginseng, Ginkgo biloba, aloe vera, grapefruit pectin, papayas, slippery elm bark, alfalfa, peppermint, and ginger tea. You can take capsules or use the ingredients to make tea, but be sure to consult your physician before using any of these substances. You can also drink lemon water, exercise strenuously, take a sauna, get a vigorous massage, and eat a high-fiber, cleansing diet. Deep breathing exercises, in clean environments, will infuse your brain with fresh oxygen. When it comes to minimizing food contaminants, wash all fruits and vegetables thoroughly.

Puzzle 2.04
Crossword

Across

1. Author Fleming
3. "You betcha!"
5. Source of iron
7. Idaho's capital
8. Swashbuckler Flynn
10. Sister of Zsa Zsa
12. Chicken ___ king
13. "___ Haw"
15. Dress down
19. "Dancing Queen" quartet
20. Actress Russo
21. Macaroni shape
23. Stick up
24. Form 1040 issuer
25. Lyricist Gershwin
27. Beast of burden
29. Noodles
33. Golden rule preposition
34. Sling mud at
35. Take a load off
36. Chest material
40. Furthermore
42. "Much ___ About Nothing"
43. King Kong, e.g.
45. Climber's goal
46. Dressed to the ___
47. Fork over
48. ___ kwon do

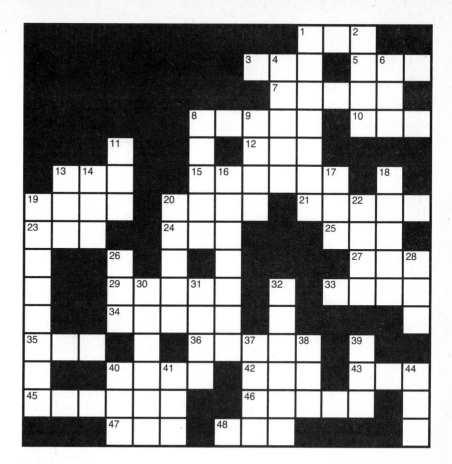

Down

1. Cut off
2. It smells
4. Deadly virus
6. Gun, as an engine
8. Hot coal
9. Steak order
11. Arthur of "The Golden Girls"
13. "The Sopranos" network
14. Flow's partner
16. Trap
17. ___ Lilly & Co.
18. Seashore
19. Location of Bill Clinton's Hope
20. Washer cycle
22. Muffin choice
26. Photo ___ (media events)
28. Beaver, to Ward
30. Aviator Earhart
31. Snack in a shell
32. Band aide
37. Comedian Carvey
38. Director Howard
39. Tank filler
40. Sound booster
41. Hog haven
44. Electric fish

Puzzle 2.05
Sudoku

		9	8	7	5	2		
		4		3		5		
3		5				9		7
1			9	4	2			8
			7	1	3			
4			5	8	6			2
5		2				8		4
		8		9		1		
		1	3	5	8	7		

Puzzle 2.06
Sudoku

		7	9	6	2	4		
9				1				2
	1		8	5	3		6	
5			4	7	9			1
				8				
4			3	2	1			7
	9		2	4	8		5	
6				3				8
		8	6	9	5	1		

Puzzle 2.07
Word Search

ALLEN IVERSON
ANDRE AGASSI
ARNOLD PALMER
ARTHUR ASHE
BARRY BONDS
BEN HOGAN
BORIS BECKER
DEION SANDERS
FRAN TARKENTON
FUZZY ZOELLER
HONUS WAGNER
ISIAH THOMAS
JACK NICKLAUS
JACKIE ROBINSON
JOE THEISMANN
JOHNNY UNITAS
JULIUS ERVING
KAREEM ABDUL JABBAR
LARRY BIRD
MAGIC JOHNSON
MICHAEL JORDAN
PATRICK EWING
PETE ROSE
PEYTON MANNING
REGGIE MILLER
ROD LAVER
SAM SNEAD
TED WILLIAMS
TERRY BRADSHAW
TOM SEAVER
WALTER PAYTON
WILT CHAMBERLAIN

```
L M A G I C J O H N S O N M L N A Y D R
J O H N N Y U N I T A S C A O H B K A E
S M A I L L I W D E T F R T N M A R E V
X S D N O B Y R R A B R Y O X R K E N A
I N G N N H Q T D G Y A S R E H E N S L
F N N A I N L W A B P N V E A R H G M D
U A I M H R W C I R I T M K R E M A A O
Z M W N I A L R E B M A H C T L I W S R
Z S E O H M D T O E B R K E H L C S R S
Y I K T J O L R S D I K R B U I H U E U
Z E C Y S A E O U S A E U S R M A N D A
O H I E W I R L S N V N Q I A E E O N L
E T R P K E J A A A J T V R S I L H A K
L E T C T A G G E Y R O J O H G J N S C
L O A E B A O S C M V N N B E G O U N I
E J P B E H M O A L L E N I V E R S O N
R Y A R N O L D P A L M E R D R D U I K
P R D E T T E R R Y B R A D S H A W E C
N N B R G Y J U L I U S E R V I N G D A
A S A M O H T H A I S I B I X O E D K J
```

Puzzle 2.08
Double Scramble

Building Block

ICBAS   _____

SIEAR   _____

MARKA   _____

ADINI   _____

AOCGR   _____

_____

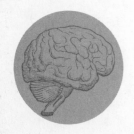

Eat More Blackberries

These dark-colored berries are loaded with powerful antioxidants and are a great fruit to add to your diet. In particular, the antioxidants known as polyphenols and anthocyanins have been associated with a healthy urinary tract and reduced risk of certain cancers, and may help protect memory function and cells. A 2009 Tufts University study also suggests that blackberries may encourage communication between neurons and improve your ability to soak up new information.

Puzzle 2.09
Provider

3 LETTERS

AGO
AIL
ALE
ATT
BAA
DAM
DOE
EKE
HEM
HUT
LEA
LIS
OHS
ORE
OSE
PAN
PIU
POI
PSI
SAC
SET
SUM
TAN
TIC
UTA

4 LETTERS

ACME
AERO
AGUE
ALAE
ALOE
APER
ARBS
AWLS
BABA
BIKE
CENT
ETAS
HEAT
LABS
LAPS
LASS
MANO
MASH
MAST
OLDS
PARS
REES
RICE
SAME
SEER
SHMO
SOCK
SOLE
STOA
STOW
SUES
TAPS
TASS
TEED
TEES
TOME
TROT
TSKS

5 LETTERS

MARES
MATER
SCARS
START
TACET
TASTE
TORTS

Puzzle 2.10
Cryptoquote

UOBF KFP HNJD EFYNQBF HAFG ANWF BCKFHAOPX

HC BNG; SCCJB, EFYNQBF HAFG ANWF HC BNG

BCKFHAOPX.

—ZJNHC

Hint: The word "fools" is found in the quote.

Puzzle 2.11
Cryptoquote

GRGDBJSRN WVEIT SO DSMZ HSOOZLCSRN G YTIN.

YZP QZIQDZ GTZ SRCZTZOCZH GRH CWZ YTIN

HSZO IY SC.

—Z.K. PWSCZ

Hint: The word "interested" is found in the quote.

Puzzle 2.12
Crossword

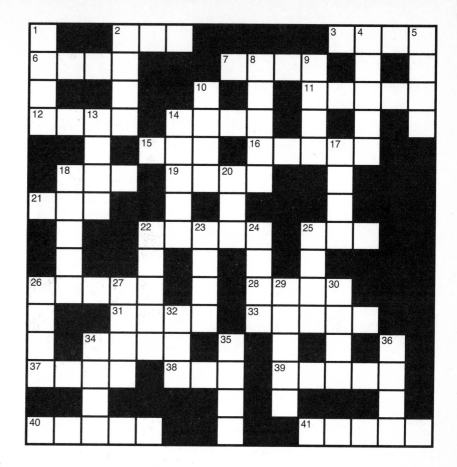

Across

2. Dove's sound
3. Put in the hold
6. Sharpen
7. Land measure
11. Come to terms
12. Try out
14. Big brass horn
15. Egyptian boy king
16. Soothing ointment
18. Wray of "King Kong"
19. Earring site
21. Mary ___ cosmetics
22. Sierra Nevada resort
25. Prohibition
26. Rocker John
28. Scored 100 on
31. Foxx of "Sanford and Son"
33. Alma ___
34. Prefix with physics or physical
37. Low digits
38. "i" completer
39. Prepared
40. Gymnast Comaneci
41. West Pointer

Down

1. Close
2. Penny
4. ___ Haute, Ind.
5. Small songbird
8. Discontinue
9. ___ of Sandwich
10. Car
13. Do in, as a dragon
14. Oklahoma city
17. MasterCard rival
18. Deadly
20. Sis's sib
22. Basic belief
23. Ranch worker
24. Checkup
25. Sugar source
26. Prepare for publication
27. Miners' finds
29. Egypt's capital
30. ___ vu
32. Pops
34. Honey drink
35. Leave speechless
36. Jekyll's alter ego

Puzzle 2.13
Sudoku

1			3	7	6			4
7								5
6		8	4	5	1	3		9
			7	6	9			
		3		2		8		
			1	3	8			
4		1	6	8	7	5		2
3								6
5			9	1	3			8

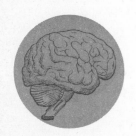

Alternate Workouts

A well-rounded exercise regimen should strengthen muscles, benefit the heart and lungs, and build endurance. For optimum results, alternate weight training, aerobics, and circuit training. Reliance on only one form of exercise will not benefit your entire body. Vary your activities to ensure a complete workout. Weight lifting strengthens your muscles and may help you lose that dangerous belly fat; you'll also need some cardiovascular activity, such as aerobics, to benefit your heart and lungs—and thus your circulatory system and blood flow to your brain. Before starting an exercise program be sure to consult your physician.

Puzzle 2.14
Double Scramble

Earthling

HYBBO   _____

MRALA   _____

NAUBR   _____

IHNTG   _____

MPEAL   _____

_____

Puzzle 2.15
Double Scramble

Log Home

AINHC   _____

XINED   _____

ENAGT   _____

EBCHA   _____

NRHTO   _____

_____

Puzzle 2.16
Sudoku

1	4		2	9			6	
6	9	8			3	4		
7		9					4	
4			5		8			7
	6					3		5
		5	6			7	8	3
	8			3	9		5	4

Puzzle 2.17
Sudoku

		8				3	5	
		4		6				9
	9		4				6	
		7		4			3	2
9		3		2		1		7
2	8			1		9		
	7				3		9	
3				7		2		
	6	2				5		

needle	baby
shoe	wing
stamp	moon
map	engine
tooth	ship

Puzzle 2.18
Forget Me Not

_____   _____

_____   _____

_____   _____

_____   _____

_____   _____

What Was Your Time?

If you decided to challenge yourself further and time your puzzling session, be sure to write down your results below. Take a moment to reflect on your past sessions and acknowledge any improvements made along the way. With every chapter in this book, you should be able to notice how much more focused and alert your brain is becoming.

_____

_____

_____

_____

_____

_____

_____

_____

_____

_____

_____

_____

_____

_____

_____

_____

CHAPTER 3

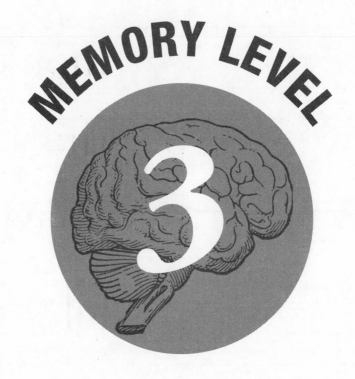

MEMORY LEVEL

3

hair	boy
cloud	monkey
bell	ring
pig	office
toe	pipe

Puzzle 3.01
Forget Me Not

_____

_____

_____

_____

_____

Puzzle 3.02
Provider

3 LETTERS

AGA	ION
AIM	MAE
AIR	MOW
ALB	ONS
BAT	OWE
BEL	PAT
BEN	RAT
BOO	SOL
EEL	SUE
ELL	TAE
ENG	TEL
ERS	THE
HON	WAR

4 LETTERS

ABBE	FONT
ALIT	GLEE
AMAS	HAST
ANSA	HATE
ANTS	HINT
ARCS	HOAR
AWAY	LADS
BEST	LAIR
CHIA	LOWE
DOGE	MEAT
ELMS	OSES
ERGO	SERE
ETHS	SHOP
EYES	SIRE
FOES	SLUE

SORA	TONE
STAT	TOPE
SWAT	TORO

5 LETTERS

GIROS	SARIS
LASER	SETTS
PEASE	SHALT
RESET	STAFF

Puzzle 3.03
Cryptoquote

NGHOECQ ND X CNL, X ZNNT EO X SXK'O ZQOH

DWEQKC. EKOECQ ND X CNL, EH EO HNN CXWT

HN WQXC.

— LWNGUFN SXWJ

Hint: The word "friend" is found in the quote.

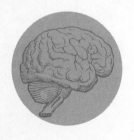

Use Essential Oils
....

Today, people all over the world are paying attention to the healing effects of essential oils, and scientists are continuing to conduct research in an attempt to understand more about the effects of these amazing aromas on the human mind, body, and psychology. Essential oils are extracted from the aromatic essences of certain plants, trees, fruits, flowers, herbs, and spices. Natural volatile oils, they have identifiable chemical and medicinal properties. Try lighting a scented candle as you relax after a hard day's work, or place fragrant potpourri throughout your home. You can even place a few drops of scented oils in your water while you relax in a hot bath or a few drops of scented oil on your pillow to help you unwind and fall asleep faster at night. The important thing is to select a fragrance that is both appealing and relaxing. Before you start experimenting with these oils, make sure you discuss their use with your physician, as some oils may not be best for your body and may cause an allergic reaction.

Puzzle 3.04
Crossword

Across

1. Nets
3. Egg ___ yung
6. Martini garnish
8. Shoe bottom
10. Puerto ___
12. Hatchling's home
16. Fat in a can
18. Brewer's need
20. Use a swizzle stick
22. Walkie-talkie word
23. Inquire
25. Waste maker
27. Got wind of
28. "Full Metal Jacket" setting, for short
30. Japanese cartoon art
33. Back talk
34. "Alley ___!"
35. Take in or let out
37. Fall from grace
38. Vintner's vessel
39. Writer Hemingway
41. Tropical weather disturbance
42. Kyoto cash

Down

1. American ___, Massachusetts state tree
2. Burn the surface of
3. Elevator stop
4. Black gold
5. Baker's need
6. Academy Awards
7. "La Dolce ___"
9. Dripping
11. Homeric epic
13. Needle hole
14. Tranquil
15. Bills
17. Buck's mate
19. Fraud
21. Flourish
24. Hang on to
26. Hiker's path
29. Excuse
31. Telegraph code name
32. Exhausted
34. Unseat
36. Short and to the point
38. Tape player
40. Like a wallflower

Puzzle 3.05
Sudoku

1		8	4	6	3	7		9
				2				
2			1		8			3
5	6		7		4		3	8
				1				
7	1		3		2		6	4
6			8		9			5
				5				
8		5	2	4	7	6		1

Puzzle 3.06
Sudoku

	3	5	9	2	4	1	7	
		2	3	8	7	6		
5		1		6		2		7
		7		4		8		
3		6		9		5		1
		3	4	5	6	9		
	5	8	1	7	9	4	3	

Puzzle 3.07
Word Search

ALBANIA
ANDORRA
ANGOLA
BELGIUM
BHUTAN
BULGARIA
CAPE VERDE
CHAD
CONGO
CROATIA
DENMARK
ETHIOPIA
FINLAND
GHANA
GREECE
INDIA
INDONESIA
LESOTHO
LIBERIA
LITHUANIA
LUXEMBOURG
MALAYSIA
MALDIVES
MALI
MONGOLIA
NAMIBIA
NETHERLANDS
NORTH KOREA
NORWAY
PORTUGAL
RWANDA
SAN MARINO

SEYCHELLES
SINGAPORE
SLOVAKIA
SOUTH KOREA
SRI LANKA
SUDAN
SWITZERLAND
TOGO
TUNISIA
TURKMENISTAN
UKRAINE
UNITED KINGDOM
YUGOSLAVIA

```
R N D O X P M A L A Y S I A I R E B I L
H A N G O L A F Y U G O S L A V I A G K
R T G O A L S X I H X N O R W A Y A E T
D U H T B I V S L N P E U F A D N A W R
E H A A M J R L B O L S M Z I Z E P L N
N B N I R I S A R X E A N B L X T N I K
M I A K L G O T G L I O N E O V H X T J
A G I A X H U X L L R X Y D G U E U H V
R U N V U G T E A T U M U R N Y R S U S
K K D O A Z H M H V U B P E O K L G A G
A R O L L C K K O I I S W V M Z A E N T
I K N S Y M O D G N I K D E T I N U I T
B U E E P R R L D N A I N P B A D U A Y
I O S J E Z E I G B I I N A D U S K R W
M B I A Y B A A O C S W P C U X Z R R Q
A D A H C X P K R T J C R O A T I A O N
N C O N G O D N A L R E Z T I W S I D O
E C E E R G O N I R A M N A S H E N N S
C D S E V I D L A M A I S I N U T E A H
I B U N D A Y I V F V X O H T O S E L N
```

Puzzle 3.08
Double Scramble

First-Anniversary Gift

LTAER   _____

CPIAN   _____

AXTEC   _____

IRPDA   _____

RTYAP   _____

_____

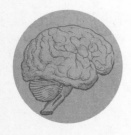

Take Potassium

Potassium is an electrolyte that works closely with its counterparts, chloride and sodium. Over 95 percent of potassium is in the body's cells and helps regulate the flow of fluids and minerals in and out of the body's cells. It also helps maintain normal blood pressure, maintain heart and kidney function, transmit nerve impulses, and control the contraction of muscles. The brain, in particular, uses this electrolyte to signal between cells, and a depletion of potassium in the body will cause lethargy. Potassium can be found in foods such as fresh meat, poultry, fish, figs, lentils, kidney beans, black beans, baked potatoes (with skin), avocados, orange juice, cantaloupes, bananas, and cooked spinach. Always consult your physician before taking mineral supplements because incorporating too much potassium into your diet may have ill effects.

Puzzle 3.09
Provider

3 LETTERS

ABS	ODE
ARK	PAM
AWL	PIA
BRR	ROE
ERE	RUE
ETH	SIR
HES	STY
IRE	TIE
LAY	TOE
LIT	TOT
MAR	TWA
OCA	WIT

4 LETTERS

ACHE	LAME
AILS	LEAR
ALAN	LOOT
ALTO	MERE
APSE	NENE
ARKS	OLES
ATOM	PICA
ATOP	RESH
BETS	SEAR
BRIT	SEEM
CHIN	SETA
COIL	SODA
ERRS	SOME
HALO	TINE
HONE	TSAR
IMAM	WIRE

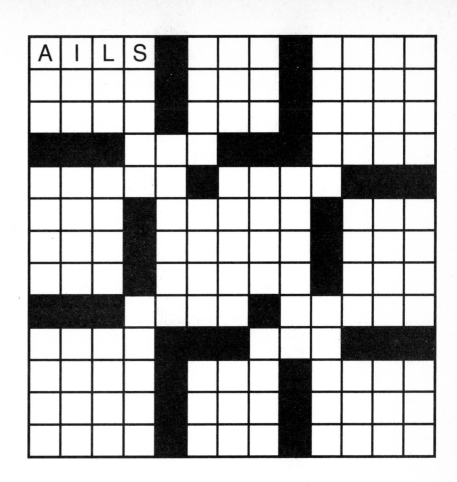

5 LETTERS

ACRES	CRASS
ALLEE	ELATE
APSES	LATHE
BEAST	METES
CLASS	STARE

6 LETTERS

RETEAR	USABLE

Puzzle 3.10
Cryptoquote

MLXU FLUJZ'W PCJW JAW WOUGU MABU V JWLZU;
AW OVJ WL NU IVFU, MABU NGUVF, GUIVFU VMM
WOU WAIU, IVFU ZUQ.

—CGJCMV B. MUKCAZ

Hint: The word "remade" is found in the quote.

Puzzle 3.11
Cryptoquote

MYBU MC WBQQ UYC ZCWOCU AX YBRRSLCZZ SZ
LA IAOC B ZCWOCU UYBL AVO MSQQSLTLCZZ UA
WYAAZC QSXC.

—QCA NVZWBTQSB

Hint: The word "secret" is found in the quote.

Puzzle 3.12
Crossword

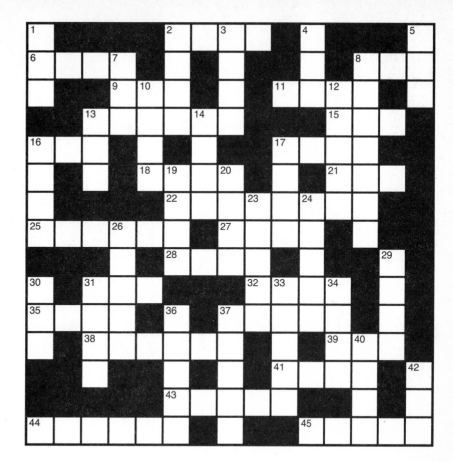

Across

2. Feel sorry for
6. Bean curd product
8. Paid player
9. California's Big ___
11. "Star Wars" sage
13. Can't stand
15. Business abbr.
16. Spelling contest
17. Gymnast Korbut
18. Enormous
21. Freezer cubes
22. Not together
25. Track down
27. "Terrible" czar
28. Art ___ (retro style)
31. Rotten
32. Shah's land, once
35. Betty of cartoons
37. Think the world of
38. "Sophie's Choice" Oscar winner
39. Wrestling surface
41. Way in or out
43. Yarns
44. Cantankerous
45. Wrapped up

Down

1. Dough dispenser?
2. Cut back
3. Pucker-producing
4. Numero ___
5. Enemy
7. Take advantage of
8. Cure-all
10. Four Corners state
12. Finger or toe
13. Dover's state: Abbr.
14. Wise guy
16. Get-out-of-jail money
17. Gumbo veggie
19. Secondhand
20. Cast-of-thousands film
23. Steer clear of
24. Egypt's Sadat
26. Go with the flow
29. Narrow opening
30. Hoops grp.
31. Head honcho
33. Highways and byways
34. Nautilus captain
36. Southpaw
37. iMac maker
40. Like the Sahara
42. Pea's place

Puzzle 3.13
Sudoku

		9	5	4	1	8		
				3				
4	8						5	1
5	3		1	9	2		8	6
			6	7	3			
7	2		4	5	8		3	9
3	6						1	5
				1				
		1	3	2	5	4		

Learn to Meditate

For eons, experts believed meditation calmed the brain, and it does, but it also activates the most thoughtful part of your brain. When you're contemplating serious matters, take time to meditate and you may find yourself making smarter decisions. How does meditation help the mind and body? Studies have found that effective meditation actually increases blood flow to the brain and balances brain wave patterns. Some studies suggest that it also boosts the immune system and improves cognitive function, including memory.

Puzzle 3.14
Double Scramble

Rodeo Rope

NGARO   _____

SMPAT   _____

SONTE   _____

AMITD   _____

ELNAR   _____

_____

Puzzle 3.15
Double Scramble

Cow Chow

UGGAE   _____

AYNIR   _____

AKENS   _____

SOONP   _____

ORCTA   _____

_____

Puzzle 3.16
Sudoku

	4		8		9			
8	1	7						4
5	6			7	8			
9		1		6				
	8		7		3		2	
			2			6		1
		4	6				9	3
2						5	4	8
			9		4	7		

Puzzle 3.17
Sudoku

	7		5					1
			2			6		5
5		3	4	1		8		
		8			4			
6		4	9		5	7		3
			7			4		
		5		4	9	2		7
3		7				2		
4					7		5	

window	curtain
sun	dress
button	collar
bee	bone
bed	horse

Puzzle 3.18
Forget Me Not

_____   _____

_____   _____

_____   _____

_____   _____

_____   _____

What Was Your Time?

If you decided to challenge yourself further and time your puzzling session, be sure to write down your results below. Take a moment to reflect on your past sessions and acknowledge any improvements made along the way. With every chapter in this book, you should be able to notice how much more focused and alert your brain is becoming.

_____

_____

_____

_____

_____

_____

_____

_____

_____

_____

_____

_____

_____

_____

_____

_____

_____

CHAPTER 4

MEMORY LEVEL 4

net	dog
pen	wire
arch	brick
finger	horn
receipt	tree

Puzzle 4.01
Forget Me Not

_____   _____

_____   _____

_____   _____

_____   _____

_____   _____

Puzzle 4.02
Provider

3 LETTERS

ADS	HOW
ALT	LAT
AMP	MAG
ATE	ONE
AVE	ORS
BUN	OUT
COO	PRO
DAY	REG
DOT	SAP
DRY	TED
HAH	TWO

4 LETTERS

AGEE	NEAT
ALBS	OGEE
ARMS	OUTS
AURA	OWES
AYES	POPS
BEEN	ROPE
COME	SABE
DADO	SANE
DEED	SCAD
EGGS	SECT
ELAN	SHAY
ETNA	SHES
HELL	SOWS
LODE	STOP
MALE	STYE
MATE	TALE

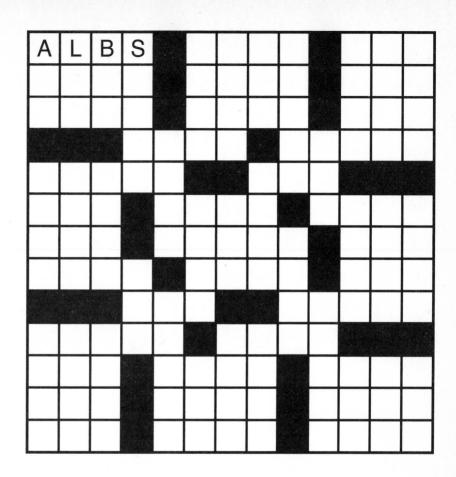

TAUT	THEE
TEEN	TYNE
THAT	WOVE

5 LETTERS

AEDES	SATES
CASTS	SCREE
LURES	SENSE
PASTE	STATE
RESTS	

Puzzle 4.03
Cryptoquote

U IVHUW SUGZ KHMKXH WPRGJ WPHZ UVH

WPRGJRGI TPHG WPHZ UVH SHVHXZ VHUVVUGIRGI

WPHRV KVHLQORNHF.

—TRXXRUS LUSHF

Hint: The word "people" is found in the quote.

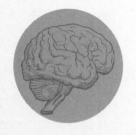

Limit Simple Sugars

Sugars are simple carbohydrates that the body uses as a source of energy. During digestion, all carbohydrates break down into sugar, or blood glucose. Some sugars occur naturally, such as in dairy products (as lactose) and fruits (as fructose). Other foods have added sugars, such as those added during processing or preparation. A high-sugar diet might interfere with optimal learning and memory functioning.

Puzzle 4.04
Crossword

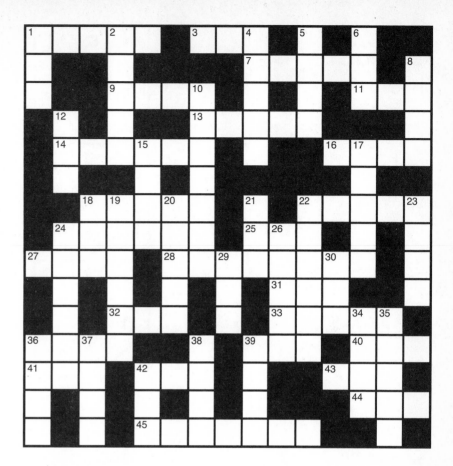

Across

1. Actress Witherspoon
3. "___ the season . . ."
7. Public square
9. Monopoly payment
11. Tell a whopper
13. Celestial hunter
14. Frank
16. Canyon comeback
18. ___ New Guinea
22. Bring together
24. Gofer's job
25. Once around the track
27. Actor Baldwin
28. South Carolina's capital
31. Wager
32. Precedes maiden name
33. Artist's stand
36. Tennis great Arthur
39. Gallery display
40. Neckline shape
41. Itsy-bitsy
42. Ginger ___
43. By way of
44. Leary's drug
45. Saddam ___

Down

1. Eminem's genre
2. Mall binge
4. Go bad
5. Conceited
6. Buddy
8. Office note
10. Transport to Oz
12. Be in the red
15. California wine valley
17. Special-occasion dishes
18. Opposite of post-
19. Esoteric
20. ___ Sam
21. Winter ailment
22. Optimistic
23. Guitarist Clapton
24. Pass, as time
26. The color of honey
29. Zodiac lion
30. Part of T.G.I.F.
34. Devil's doings
35. Minimum
36. Not home
37. Make well
38. Porgy's woman
39. Diarist Frank
42. Volcanic spew

Puzzle 4.05
Sudoku

	5	4				8	3	
1				6				7
7	8		2	3	5		4	6
	2	7				4	6	
				9				
	6	3				9	1	
2	7		1	4	6		8	9
3				2				4
	9	6				2	5	

Puzzle 4.06
Sudoku

5	3		2	9	6		8	7
		4		8		6		
			4		5			
4	7			3			2	6
		2		6		5		
6	1			2			3	9
			6		3			
		7		5		9		
1	4		8	7	9		6	5

Puzzle 4.07
Word Search

APPLE
APRICOT
ARTICHOKE
BANANA
BEET
BLACKBERRY
BOYSENBERRY
BROCCOLI
CANTALOUPE
CARROT
CAULIFLOWER
CELERY
COCONUT
CRANBERRY
CUCUMBER
FIG
GREEN BEANS
GREEN PEPPER
GUAVA
HUCKLEBERRY
KUMQUAT
LEMON
LENTILS
LETTUCE
LIME
LOGANBERRY
MELON
MULBERRY
OKRA
ONION
PAPAYA
PARSNIP

PEACH
PERSIMMON
PLUM
POTATO
PUMPKIN
RASPBERRY
SPINACH
SQUASH
TANGERINE
TURNIP
WATERCRESS
WATERMELON
YAM

```
C K M U B Y Z P A P A Y A R K O B C E H
M P E B O R R A A Y E N M P H K H D V I
Q G L E Z F G R E E N P E P P E R A W Z
L N O M M I S R E P U O L A T N A C T Q
F Z N I N N E N Y B L B P C O C O N U T
L N Z L I I I K R R N S I L O C C O R B
K G W P P R K E O L R E L P P A J L N L
O U Y A E E B P A H G E S V S D G E I O
X A M G T M A L M H C I B Y S N R M P M
A V N K U E E C A U L I F L O W E R M P
B A Y C S T R P H C P Q T V U B E E W Z
T B U R T L R C V K K O U R Y M N T C B
A C P U R I I C R L B B T H A R B A X A
U W C J C E H T E E B N E A C N E W U D
Q E R O N U B S N B S D O R T A A L X J
M Y T F L Q Q N B E G S I I R O N N E M
U X A I M U L P A R L E M O N Y S I A C
K M T A A N E Y R R E B N A G O L Y P B
K R A S P B E R R Y C A R R O T U G Z S
F U H V H Y X T I F V X L Y M D Z P P N
```

Puzzle 4.08
Double Scramble

Halloween Choice

RYPEL   _____

KYAKA   _____

ESEAT   _____

TCCAH   _____

IOTID   _____

_____

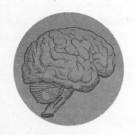

Turn Down the Noise

The most striking area in which older people and younger people differ is in their ability to multitask. In a study conducted across three generations and published in *Elsevier*, researchers found that in general, younger people are better at multitasking—that is, engaging in several functions at once—such as watching a movie on TV while cramming for a history exam. Older people, however, faced a number of mental limitations in the types of tasks that they could multitask. This study suggests that it may be advantageous to focus on only one or two tasks at a time rather than trying to tackle several at once. It also may be helpful to carry out these tasks in a quiet environment to help the brain truly focus on what needs to be completed.

Puzzle 4.09
Provider

3 LETTERS

AID
ANA
ANT
APE
BRO
ELK
ELS
ENS
EVE
HIS
LAS
LED

LEI
NAE
NOT
OHM
PAP
RID
SEN
TOM
TRY
WOO
YEA

4 LETTERS

ADDS
ALAR
ANON
AWES
AWOL
BALE
BENT
BRAG
CASE
CATS
EPEE
HOOT
ILKS
INNS
KINE
LAIN

LIEN
LION
LITE
MOTE
MYTH
NAVE
ODES
ORTS
OWNS
PERI
RIPE
SANS
SAYS
SEEN
SEMI
SKEE

SPED
TENS
TEST

TILE
TOES
TREE

5 LETTERS

ATLAS
BASER
BLAST
CASTE
GESTE

SLEET
SLICE
STEED
TEMPS

Puzzle 4.10
Cryptoquote

YN HYG JGMWZGFC WYN EZNCNMW, JGMWZGFC

WYN EKCW. YN HYG JGMWZGFC WYN EKCW,

JGMWZGFC WYN PQWQZN.

—LNGZLN GZHNFF

Hint: The word "future" is found in the quote.

Puzzle 4.11
Cryptoquote

BDMBID KUML VGUMPKG DRBDUZDWJD ZC VGDA

XDDV IZCD GMWDYVIA QWE JMPUQKDMPYIA. VGZY

ZY GML JGQUQJVDU ZY OPZIV.

—DIDQWMU UMMYDTDIV

Hint: The word "honestly" is found in the quote.

Puzzle 4.12
Crossword

Across

1. Bucks and does
5. Reunion attendee
8. Jeans material
9. Phi ___ Kappa
10. Oregon's capital
12. Border
13. Prefix with cycle or sex
14. Sharon of Israel
15. Garr of "Tootsie"
16. ___ up (come clean)
17. Go kaput
19. Vote in
22. Pepper's partner
23. Bin ___
25. Come to pass
28. British john
29. Reebok rival
31. Days of ___
33. 100 centavos
35. Make amends (for)
37. Explosive letters
38. Actor Sharif
39. Track shape
40. Final Four game
41. NASDAQ debut
43. Coffee, slangily
44. "Nova" network
45. Poke fun at
46. "___, humbug!"

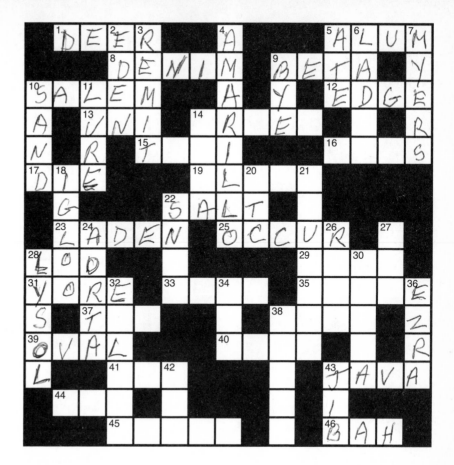

Down

2. Genesis locale
3. Send, as payment
4. Texas Panhandle city
5. Consumed
6. Soup scoop
7. Press Secretary DeeDee
    ____
9. Parting word
10. Hourglass contents
11. Tackle box item
14. Length times width
18. Ice house

20. And so on: Abbr.
21. Seaquake consequence
22. Scissors sound
24. Major artery
26. Meter maid of song
27. Barbie's beau
28. Disinfectant brand
30. "M*A*S*H" setting
32. Sign up
34. Sea plea
36. Poet Pound
38. Prophetic signs
42. Egg cells
43. Triangular sail

Puzzle 4.13
Sudoku

1	9		7		5		6	3
		7	4		6	5		
	2	5				4	7	
8		6		5		7		9
5		2		3		1		6
	6	3				9	8	
		8	3		2	6		
7	5		6		8		1	2

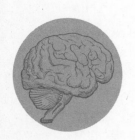

Stay Mentally Alert

The brain is affected by age. Researchers note that the brain tends to shrink an average of 6 percent over our lifetime, resulting in a loss of cognitive abilities, such as memory, problem solving, and digesting information. Forgetfulness is, without question, one of the most common "complaints" of aging, though it's more often due to reduced oxygen or a lack of use than to Alzheimer's disease or other organic disorders. Indeed, the phrase "use it or lose it" really applies to the brain; studies have found that older individuals who enjoy solving puzzles, read a lot, or regularly engage in other forms of mental stimulation tend to have better memories than those who don't. Stimulating cognitive functions can enhance them and preserve them.

Puzzle 4.14
Double Scramble

Goliath

ONISY   _____

DUALO   _____

STTAY   _____

DERAG   _____

NPUIT   _____

_____

Puzzle 4.15
Double Scramble

Not Clear

EIODV   _____

YNEME   _____

GVOLE   _____

SPEUT   _____

AGREU   _____

_____

Puzzle 4.16
Sudoku

9	5		8			4		
4			5					
	7	2	9					
2		3	1			7		4
	1			4			3	
5		9			3	6		1
					8	2	1	
					2			7
		1			7		6	8

Puzzle 4.17
Sudoku

1	5		9		7		6	8
3								5
8		7				2		4
4			1		5			3
6			3		2			1
5		4				8		6
7								2
2	8		6		4		5	9

Puzzle 4.18
Forget Me Not

sail	line
ear	skin
card	nail
cake	tail
comb	flag

Puzzle 4.18
Forget Me Not

_____   _____

_____   _____

_____   _____

_____   _____

_____   _____

What Was Your Time?

If you decided to challenge yourself further and time your puzzling session, be sure to write down your results below. Take a moment to reflect on your past sessions and acknowledge any improvements made along the way. With every chapter in this book, you should be able to notice how much more focused and alert your brain is becoming.

_____

_____

_____

_____

_____

_____

_____

_____

_____

_____

_____

_____

_____

_____

_____

_____

_____

_____

CHAPTER 5

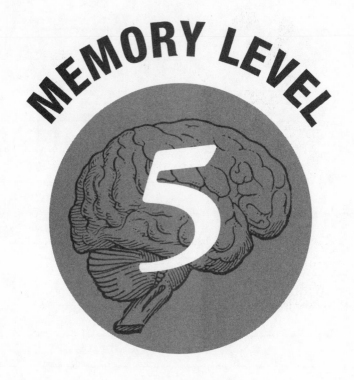

MEMORY LEVEL

Puzzle 5.01
Forget Me Not

berry

spoon

mouth

chin

ticket

spring

store

bath

house

cat

Puzzle 5.01

Forget Me Not

_____   _____

_____   _____

_____   _____

_____   _____

_____   _____

Puzzle 5.02
Provider

3 LETTERS

AMI	OAF
BAR	ODD
BOA	OFF
FEN	OHO
FIR	ORC
FLU	PEE
FOE	PIT
FRO	SIN
MID	SYN
NUN	TIS

4 LETTERS

AGIO	LIMA
AGON	MINI
AMEN	OBOE
AMIE	ORBS
BREE	ORCS
DATA	POST
DEAN	RASP
EASE	SEAT
EFFS	SHAH
FLAP	SIDE
FORE	SLID
HAMS	SNIT
HART	STET
HIDE	TAMP
IDEM	TITI
LAMP	TONS

5 LETTERS

BATON	PLATS
DENSE	RELIT
GIFTS	SNARE

6 LETTERS

AGREES	BERATE
ARISES	FREELY
ATONER	REASON

7 LETTERS

SORBETS	TASTIER

F U N I   U X   V C   Q I   F U Y I E ,   O C V   J C O V W C F F I E ,   B O E

D R L B O U V G   U X   K C O   Q G   J C O V U O R U O Z   V C   T F B G   U O

N B J I   C N   J I W V B U O   E I N I B V .

— W B F T D   I F F U X C O

Hint: The word "humanity" is found in the quote.

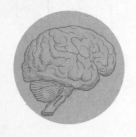

Limit Time Spent Watching Television

The reasons behind a lack of mental stimulation are many. Some people become numbed by too much television, while others dull their brains with alcohol and other stupefying substances. Prescription and over-the-counter drug interactions can also impair cognitive function, as can certain medical conditions. But for the majority of older Americans, isolation and a lack of social interaction are the primary culprits. Social support means a lot of social interaction: We chat with friends, engage in a variety of activities, and live a relatively active life. All of this stimulates the brain on a number of important levels, keeping our cognitive skills honed. But older people who lack social support often have little to do to occupy their time except watch television. As you age, make sure you keep your brain active with activities that get your body moving and stimulate your brain. You may also want to adopt a pet or care for a plant because these activities can help you stay mentally alert.

Puzzle 5.04
Crossword

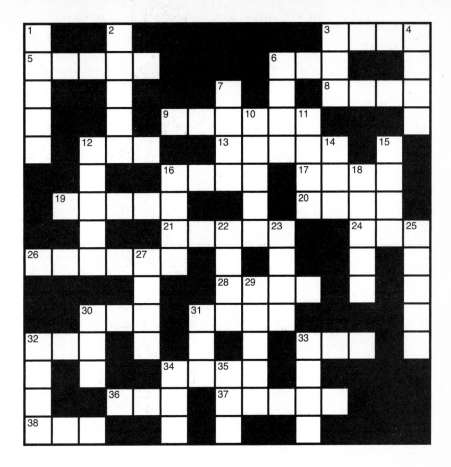

Across

3. Guys' partners
5. Scout unit
6. Ground breaker
8. Nick at ___
9. Plot
12. Sprite
13. Change, as the Constitution
16. Irene of "Fame"
17. Actress Moore
19. Kind of bean
20. Winter fall
21. String quartet member
24. Pot top
26. Thinly spread
28. Shakespearean king
30. Have a bawl
31. Lend a hand
32. To and ___
33. Decay
34. Musical chairs goal
36. ___ Aviv
37. Katmandu's land
38. Pull the plug on

Down

1. Geyser output
2. Alpine call
3. ___-Xers (boomers' kids)
4. Took to court
6. "Where the heart is"
7. Blacken
10. Internet letters
11. Wraps up
12. Author Jong
14. Bear lair
15. Fuzzy fruit
16. Shoreline recess
18. Back tooth
22. Eye up and down
23. Quickly, in memos
25. Clothesline alternative
27. River of Hades
29. Chosen few
30. Gear tooth
31. Tint
32. Kismet
33. Caboose
34. Like a fox
35. Raggedy doll

Puzzle 5.05
Sudoku

4		2	6		5	3		9
		7		4		2		
9			7		3			1
8				1				6
		4	3	5	2	1		
3				6				4
5			2		4			3
		8		3		9		
2		3	1		8	6		7

Puzzle 5.06
Sudoku

		3	9		4	6		
	8		2	1	7		9	
9			8	6	3			4
	9						6	
		7	6	2	1	3		
	6						1	
5			7	3	6			1
	7		4	8	2		3	
		8	1		5	7		

Puzzle 5.07
Word Search

ABBREVIATION
ADJECTIVE
ADVERB
APOSTROPHE
ARTICLE
CAPITALIZATION
CLAUSE
COMMA
COMPOUND
CONJUNCTION
DETERMINERS
DIAGRAMMING
EXCLAMATION MARK
FRAGMENT
HYPHEN
INFINITIVES
INTERJECTION
ITALICS
LEXICON
MODIFIER
NOUN
PARENTHESES
PARTICIPLE
PERIOD
PHRASE
PLURAL
POSSESSIVE
PREPOSITION
PRONOUN
PUNCTUATION
QUESTION MARK
QUOTATION MARKS

```
K D U V D O I R E P R O N O U N K S V N
Z O S E S E H T N E R A P G O R G E R E
I E H P O R T S O P A A N L A N R N P J
Y G N I L L E P S W R I O M I B P T H E
E G C T A W E N C T N C N M A V C E R S
K X I A R S X I I I I O M F I C A N A N
O D N L U W K C L M I A R N O N P C S E
M M F I L S I R E T R A T N F O I E E T
I N I C P P E S A G G E J B D I T V N C
V A N S L D U M A M R U T N R T A I C E
P Y I E N A A I E J N M F E W I L S O J
G R T U L L D N E C W O R D D S I S M B
Y A I C C B T C L E X I C O N Z E P U
Z L V X A R T I C L E T R T N A A S O S
Q U E S T I O N M A R K N U A R T S U V
C B S R O N O X P R E P O S I T I O N T
J A D N O I T A U T C N U P D K O P D Z
S C O M M A B B R E V I A T I O N U U X
M O D I F I E R V P M P N E H P Y H Q R
E V I T C E J D A D V E R B N H V U H Q
```

SEMICOLON
SENTENCE
SPELLING
SUBJECT
TENSE
TRANSITION
UNDERLINING
VERB
VOCABULARY
WORD

Puzzle 5.08
Double Scramble

Power Source

PAORE   _____

IREVR   _____

YEMBA   _____

ESATT   _____

LVEIO   _____

_____

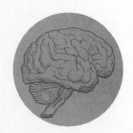

Eat Nutrient-Rich Vegetables

Vegetables are packed with all types of healthy nutrients. Daily requirements for several vitamins—including vitamin C, folic acid, and beta-carotene, the precursor for vitamin A—can be met almost exclusively from fresh vegetables and fruits. This is especially true with dark green, leafy vegetables, such as spinach, kale, or broccoli, and dark orange vegetables, such as carrots or yams. One study found that elderly people who ate nearly three servings of these vegetables a week compared to elderly people who had less than a serving of these vegetables weekly experienced a nearly 40 percent reduction in their cognitive decline over a six-year period.

Puzzle 5.09
Provider

3 LETTERS

AWE
BIO
BRA
DAP
DEW
DEY
EAT
ERN
HUH
ILL
IMP
LEE

MUG
NUT
OAT
OBI
ORT
PAR
RIP
SAD
SHY
SOU
USE

4 LETTERS

AIRY
ALBA
AMAH
BOOB
COBB
CREW
EBBS
ECHO
ERAS
EWER
FEAR
FETA
ISMS
LADE
LARS
LOUT

LUGS
ODDS
OWLS
PFFT
PIPS
PLED
PREP
PYRE
RAIN
REAP
ROTO
SEES
SEWN
SHIP
SHOO
SLAP

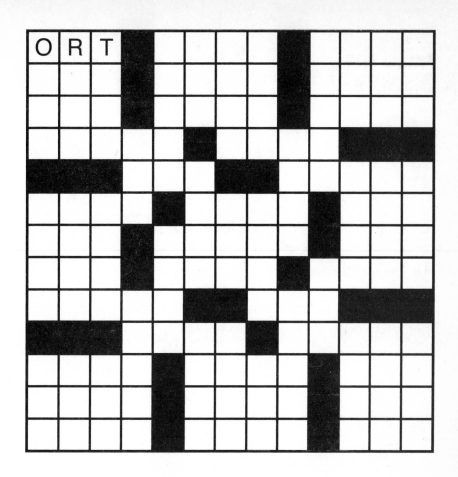

SOAP
SPAR
SPOT

SPRY
TUBA
TYPE

5 LETTERS

BESTS
CHAOS
DRAPE
IDLES
PASSE

PASTS
POSTS
RIANT
SPENT

Puzzle 5.10
Cryptoquote

EW NFW CNAW EJBW IPO LG OKW FWDPZZWDOJPI

PS PYF QNBO, LYO LG OKW FWBQPIBJLJZJOG SPF

PYF SYOYFW.

—TWPFTW LWFINFA BKNE

Hint: The word "responsibility" is found in the quote.

Puzzle 5.11
Cryptoquote

XIMV RWT MZVB ZG GUBJC CTOZJN CR VZJE

GRPBCXZJN CR ER DZCX CXB CZPB DB XIHB

TWGXBE CXTRWNX MZVB CTOZJN CR GIHB.

—DZMM TRNBTG

Hint: The word "rushed" is found in the quote.

Puzzle 5.12
Crossword

Across

4. Appear to be
6. Polynesian carving
7. Wheel shaft
9. Apollo destination
10. Shell game, e.g.
12. Part of CNN
13. Fortuneteller's card
15. Respond to reveille
17. Light bulb, in comics
19. Playing marble
20. ___ d'oeuvre
21. Weaving machine
23. Simple
25. Part to play
26. Unwanted e-mail
28. Loch ___
30. It may be checkered
32. "___ Well That Ends Well"
33. In ___ straits
34. Trade
35. ___ Mahal
36. Cacophony
37. Soccer legend

Down

1. Office fill-in
2. Cloud number
3. Snake sound
5. Photo finish
6. Cereal box tiger
8. Enticed
11. Indian corn
14. "___ the night before . . ."
15. Accumulate
16. Flower holder
17. Composer Stravinsky
18. Bloke
21. True-blue
22. "___ Lisa"
24. Cain's brother
26. Shoe material
27. Open a crack
29. Pan-fry
31. "The final frontier"

Puzzle 5.13
Sudoku

1	8		9		2		3	7
	7						9	
6			8	3	7			4
2	4						6	9
		5	4		9	2		
7	9						5	8
8			6	7	1			3
	3						2	
4	1		2		3		8	5

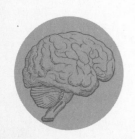

Fall in Love

According to Dr. Frank Lawlis in *The IQ Answer*, falling in love stimulates your brain. "The act of loving someone can be directly observed through the brain and throughout your body. Your immune system sparkles with excitement that creates a better defense against disease, and you actually gain muscular strength. Your creativity soars from the stimulation of the right brain so even males begin to integrate their intellectual vision with creativity." He suggests that building a relationship with a partner or strengthening an already existing relationship may help you improve your health, and thus, ensure that your brain functions at its best.

Puzzle 5.14
Double Scramble

Chubby Checker's Dance

EWLHE   _____

EHTNT   _____

OHRST   _____

LOIOG   _____

HCAET   _____

_____

Puzzle 5.15
Double Scramble

Soft Drink Size

BUMHT   _____

DVLEO   _____

GEAMI   _____

YREMH   _____

BONYE   _____

_____

Puzzle 5.16
Sudoku

7		8	5	4				
		4	8					6
3		5	6		9			7
						3		2
			9		4			
5		7						
4			7		5	6		3
9					1	7		
				9	3	2		1

Puzzle 5.17
Sudoku

			6		5			
8		5	2		4	9		7
3		2	7		8	1		6
1		7				6		5
2		6				4		9
4		8	3		9	7		1
9		1	4		2	5		3
			8		1			

wall

ant

blade

rail

cheese

garden

clock

town

cup

drain

Puzzle 5.18
Forget Me Not

_____   _____

_____   _____

_____   _____

_____   _____

_____   _____

What Was Your Time?

If you decided to challenge yourself further and time your puzzling session, be sure to write down your results below. Take a moment to reflect on your past sessions and acknowledge any improvements made along the way. With every chapter in this book, you should be able to notice how much more focused and alert your brain is becoming.

_____

_____

_____

_____

_____

_____

_____

_____

_____

_____

_____

_____

_____

_____

_____

CHAPTER 6

MEMORY LEVEL

Puzzle 6.01
Forget Me Not

basket	brush
thumb	glove
face	door
skirt	tongue
oven	root

Puzzle 6.01
Forget Me Not

_____   _____

_____   _____

_____   _____

_____   _____

_____   _____

Puzzle 6.02

Provider

3 LETTERS

ALS	INK
AMA	LEG
ANI	MAN
AVA	NOW
BET	OOH
ERR	OPS
FAN	PRY
FEY	RAW
GOO	REF
HET	TEA
HUE	TEN
ICE	

4 LETTERS

AAHS	LOGE
ACES	METE
ACRE	NOSE
ARCO	OARS
AUNT	OFFS
BIER	PEAT
BRAT	PEKE
BYES	PROA
CAPS	RAFT
CHIS	REAR
EAVE	SALE
FLEE	SEAS
GLUE	SERF
GNAT	SHOE
ICES	SONE
LATE	SPIN

SYNE	TOOT
TART	TWAS
TETS	TWIN

5 LETTERS

ANGST	PUMAS
BASSO	SABLE
COLTS	STEAL
EASES	STENO
NOTES	

Puzzle 6.03
Cryptoquote

CVO VHGGAOMC SPSOQCM PX SI TAXO VHYO

NOOQ CVO XOK KVALV A VHYO GHMMOU HC VPSO

AQ CVO NPMPS PX SI XHSATI.

—CVPSHM BOXXOWMPQ

Hint: The word "moments" is found in the quote.

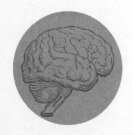

Eat More Chocolate

In a study done by Salk Institute researcher Henriette van Praag and colleagues, a compound found in cocoa, epicatechin, combined with exercise, was found to promote functional changes in a part of the brain involved in the formation of learning and memory. Epicatechin is one of a group of chemicals called flavonols, which have previously been shown to improve cardiovascular function and increase blood flow to the brain. Dr. van Praag's findings suggest a diet rich in flavonoids could help reduce the effects of neurodegenerative illnesses, such as Alzheimer's disease, or cognitive disorders related to aging.

Puzzle 6.04
Crossword

Across

2. Rock's Bon ___
3. Run in neutral
6. ___mart
7. Squirrel away
11. One of the Three Bears
13. Cast out
15. Scent
16. Consumed
18. Stubble remover
20. Accord maker
24. Fly like an eagle
25. Hairless
27. Stir-fry pan
28. Utopian
29. Take care of
31. ___ Strauss & Co.
32. Singer Turner
33. Party handout
34. Carnival city
35. Yo-Yo Ma's instrument
36. Lose traction

Down

1. Thunder sound
2. Holy war
4. Sandwich shop
5. Out of this world
8. Broadcast
9. Letter starter
10. Paraphernalia

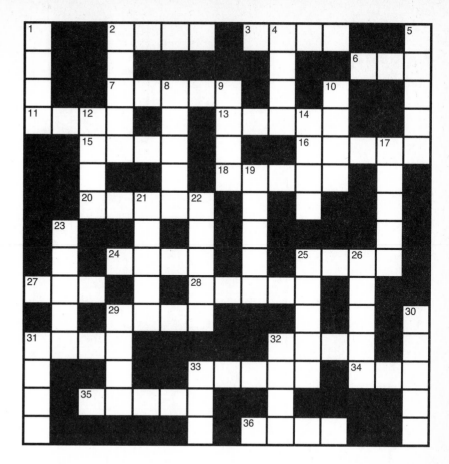

12. Ritzy
14. Ponce de ___
17. Urged (___ on)
19. Unescorted
21. Lasso loop
22. Sharp-smelling
23. Bullwinkle, for one
25. Britain's Tony
26. Kind of eclipse
29. Fork prong
30. Pueblo material
31. Fibber
32. Clock sound with tick
33. Henhouse raider

Puzzle 6.05
Sudoku

		3		1		8		
2				6				3
6	9			5			2	1
7		6	1	8	4	3		2
			2		5			
1		2	3	9	6	5		7
8	2			3			7	9
9				4				6
		4		2		1		

Puzzle 6.06
Sudoku

	8		5	3	2		4	
4				6				1
2	3		4		7		5	8
6	5						7	3
			3		5			
3	9						1	5
9	6		2		3		8	7
7				4				9
	2		7	9	1		6	

Puzzle 6.07
Word Search

ACID RAIN
BLOWING SNOW
CLEAR
CLIMATE
CLOUDY
COLD
CYCLONE
DEW
DRIZZLE
DUST STORM
FLOOD
FOG
FREEZING RAIN
FROST
HAIL
HURRICANE
ICE STORM
LIGHTNING
METEOROLOGIST
MIST
PRECIPITATION
RAINBOW
RAINFALL
SLEET
SNOWFALL
TEMPERATURE
THUNDER
TORNADO
TYPHOON
WEATHER BALLOON
WEATHER VANE
WINDSOCK
WINDY

```
D J L E W O P D T Z S J X P H W K R W B
E I G O P H L Q Q H W W R M P X N W L G
E B V O K O S Z X N I A R D I C A S W F
L W C E C Y H Y Y D U O L C T G G I O A
X L I W O Q R U P T T X T S O R F G B K
I W A N S E W O N S G N I W O L B J N L
U N Y F D F K C T B S G N I N T H G I L
E O N N N Y X S S N O W F A L L J J A S
J O U O I I U J R L T M C Q N C M T R Z
H H Z U W D A A O E R R B O I W E O T Q
T P X K T V E R E O B P M Q A J N R U N
A Y I A E L O L W E A T H E R V A N E O
R T A I C E S T O R M J V R G N C A N D
T W E A T H E R B A L L O O N L I D O R
T P R E C I P I T A T I O N I K R O L I
T F M G B J D V T O U E Z M Z W R B C Z
B X J A L L T Q H S S K A S E L U Z Y Z
V A D D O O N D W K I T Y D E I H P C L
G F R Y J P R J M T E M P E R A T U R E
H W F U T B A V V S D O O L F H X U Z B
```

Puzzle 6.08
Double Scramble

Coffee Sweetener

EUGST   _____

PLYPA   _____

RGTHI   _____

ESNEV   _____

ERCUL   _____

_____

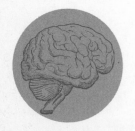

Attend Lectures

Lectures offer incredible opportunities to learn, acquire new interests, stay current, and improve your conversational skills. Pick topics that you know nothing about—like neuroscience, archeology, quantum physics, ancient history, hieroglyphics, etc.—and charge up your brain cells by straining to understand. The more complex the subject matter, the more it generates new thoughts and gets your brain waves sparking.

Puzzle 6.09
Provider

3 LETTERS

AFT   LYE
BOY   NEE
CAW   PIE
DID   RAN
EGO   REM
EMS   RES
ERG   RHO
GAM   RUM
GNU   TSK
HMM   UGH

4 LETTERS

ABLE   PURR
ACTS   REAM
AGAR   REPO
AGHA   ROOM
ALOW   SEEK
ARID   SLAW
BERG   SNOW
BURG   SNUG
CITE   SOIL
COON   TAME
FLAT   TEDS
FOYS   TIRE
ILIA   TIRO
MATT   TORA
MIND   TYES
NORM   WING

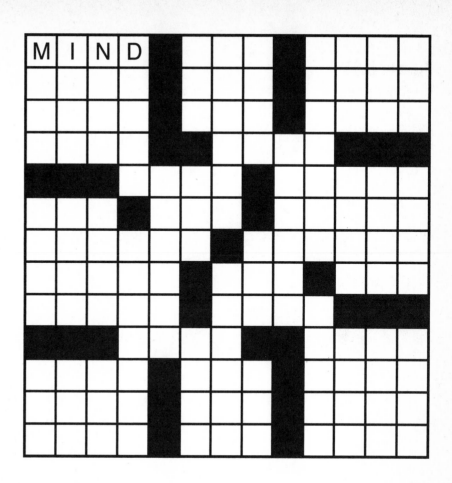

5 LETTERS

DWEEB   MELEE
EDGES   RIFTS
MASTS   TINEA

6 LETTERS

ARMADA   MANAGE
DROGUE   PARADE
IRISES   UNEASE

7 LETTERS

BARRIER   SEERESS

Puzzle 6.10
Cryptoquote

WVS QXKB XJ XWJ PUK GRNYS, NKB XK XWJSRM,

YNK QNDS VSNHSK PM VSRR, NKB N VSRR PM

VSNHSK.

—EPVK QXRWPK

Hint: The word "place" is found in the quote.

Puzzle 6.11
Cryptoquote

APXNET XEE VPA RXA DIXAK XKOPNDBIT, LQI BM

TGQ CXAI IG IPDI X VXA'D RUXNXRIPN, SBOP UBV

FGCPN.

—XLNXUXV EBARGEA

Hint: The word "adversity" is found in the quote.

Puzzle 6.12
Crossword

Across

2. Mao ___-tung
5. Take five
8. Wild blue yonder
10. Ready for business
13. Make into law
15. ___ out a living
17. Go it alone
18. ___ Solo of "Star Wars"
19. Call on
20. Part of UNLV
22. ___ sapiens
25. Love, Italian-style
28. Storm preceder
30. No-win situation
31. Least costly
33. Clear the blackboard
35. Sagan of "Cosmos"
36. ___ Beta Kappa
38. "___ we there yet?"
39. Singer Cara
40. "Tickle Me" Muppet doll
42. Venus de ___
44. Pop singer Tori
45. Costa ___
47. Long ___ and far away
48. Vintage
49. Medicine-approving org.
50. ___ Baba

Down

1. Mass ___
3. Take to court
4. Atlantis, Endeavor or Discovery, e.g.
6. Beach souvenir
7. ___ Ness monster
9. Ukraine's capital
11. School org.
12. ___ Moines
14. Ark builder
16. Fate
21. World Cup sport
23. ___-jongg
24. Grand ___ Opry
25. Bridal path
26. Loaded
27. Soccer star Hamm
29. PC alternative
30. Intense fear
32. Jack and Jill's vessel
33. Adam's madam
34. ___ Paulo, Brazil
36. Praline nut
37. Baghdad resident
41. Fall behind
42. Cattle call?
43. ___ of Man
44. Tack on
46. Under the weather

Puzzle 6.13
Sudoku

2	6	7	5		1	4	9	3
1								2
9			7		2			8
	5	3				2	8	
				4				
	9	1				6	4	
7			8		6			5
5								6
3	8	6	2		7	9	1	4

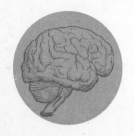

Throw Away the Grocery List

A good memory trick is to turn a grocery run into a game. After you've made a written list of your needs, memorize it to the best of your ability by taking a mental walk through your kitchen and pantry. Shop without referring to the list and see how well you've done before checking out. If your memory is sharp, you'll probably be able to remember almost everything. Since you shop for groceries often, this simple exercise will have a cumulative effect.

Puzzle 6.14
Double Scramble

Kind of Eclipse

LVEEL _____

OVABE _____

OUNNI _____

RDAYE _____

SONIE _____

_____

Puzzle 6.15
Double Scramble

Moola

YAISD _____

DEREL _____

AAYRR _____

EBCNH _____

ARNVE _____

_____

Puzzle 6.16
Sudoku

9	8					1	5	7
1	5				7	4		8
		7						
6	9			2				3
			6		9			
4				3			6	1
						3		
3		2	9				7	5
8	7	9					1	4

Puzzle 6.17
Sudoku

3	4		8				5	1
			3			2		
8				4				6
	3	5		7				4
			6		3			
6				5		7	3	
4				2				7
		9			6			
1	2				9		6	3

flame   cord

flower   machine

comb   key

change   water

bridge   collar

Puzzle 6.18
Forget Me Not

_____   _____

_____   _____

_____   _____

_____   _____

_____   _____

What Was Your Time?

If you decided to challenge yourself further and time your puzzling session, be sure to write down your results below. Take a moment to reflect on your past sessions and acknowledge any improvements made along the way. With every chapter in this book, you should be able to notice how much more focused and alert your brain is becoming.

_____

_____

_____

_____

_____

_____

_____

_____

_____

_____

_____

_____

_____

_____

_____

_____

_____

CHAPTER 7

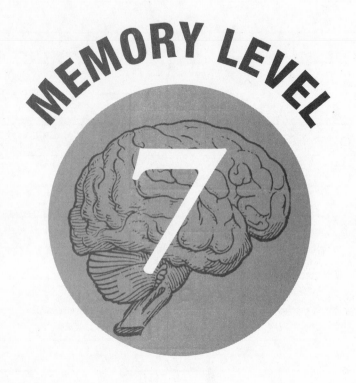

MEMORY LEVEL 7

Puzzle 7.01
Forget Me Not

plough	needle
tongue	skirt
blade	cheese
chin	pump
cake	wall

Puzzle 7.01
Forget Me Not

_____   _____

_____   _____

_____   _____

_____   _____

_____   _____

Puzzle 7.02
Provider

3 LETTERS

ABA	HIE
ABO	KIN
ACE	LAD
AND	NOS
ANY	OPE
BAD	OUR
BAL	PEN
BOD	PIG
BYE	RAY
DIE	SHA
EFT	SPY
GAR	YES

4 LETTERS

AEON	LENO
ANDS	MOOR
ANIL	OPTS
AVES	PETS
BABE	PILE
BAGS	PRIG
BAKE	PUPA
BEND	RENT
CARD	SAGA
CUBE	SNAG
DADS	SPAN
DYNE	TERN
EDGE	TREY
FIAT	UVEA
GIRT	WHYS
HEAR	YOGI

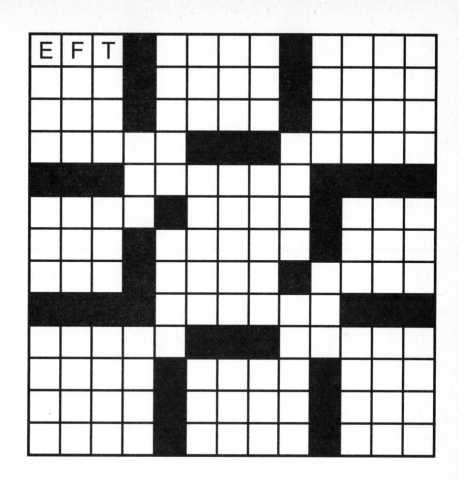

5 LETTERS

AGGIE	RILLE
ETNAS	SLASH
GREEN	STELE
OGLES	TEMPT
PESTS	WASPS

6 LETTERS

CHARGE	TEENSY

Puzzle 7.03
Cryptoquote

ZP LPG CPAAPM MSDFD GSD IVGS WVR ADVZ. JP

HLOGDVZ MSDFD GSDFD HO LP IVGS VLZ ADVKD

V GFVHA.

—FVAIS MVAZP DWDFOPL

Hint: The word "instead" is found in the quote.

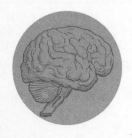

Be Creative

Creativity goes beyond thinking, beyond the gathering and assimilation of information. Creativity is what happens in your brain when you relax and allow your brain to birth new thoughts, new ways of seeing, or new ways of doing. According to Dr. Frank Lawlis, author of *The IQ Answer*, when we focus on problems, we use our brains to establish "rational relationships and cogent associations." Dr. Lawlis says a problem-solving brain emits LoBeta waves, indicative of the process of transferring information from one area of the brain to another. When you enter a creative state, however, Dr. Lawlis believes your brain enters the Theta state in which your frontal lobe shuts down, allowing other lobes to light up. In this creative state, the occipital lobe (imagery) and the temporal lobe (memory) activate. In effect, your brain goes into a sort of blissful, hypnotic state that often results in creative works of art.

Puzzle 7.04
Crossword

Across

1. Bottomless pit
6. Snake charmer's snake
7. Thailand, once
8. Pay tribute to
9. Wrinkle remover
10. Paul Bunyan's tool
11. CD-___
12. "Star Wars" director
17. Tarzan's transport
18. Headed for overtime
19. Uncle ___
21. Urban haze
23. Salty sauce
25. Tuckered out
27. Slugger Williams
28. Eat away at
29. Cub Scout groups
30. Opening for a coin
33. Artist Picasso
35. Quote
36. Relocate
37. Window ledge
38. Field yield
39. Iowa State city

Down

1. Tummy trouble
2. Beat it
3. Up to the job
4. Japanese verse
5. Tonic's partner
7. Soft drink
11. ___ Tin Tin
13. Diet guru Jenny
14. Transmits
15. Foe
16. Hertz competitor
18. Dog in Oz
20. Concert venue
21. Witnessed
22. Red planet
24. Nabisco cookie
26. "___ we forget . . ."
29. ___ Perignon
31. Not as much
32. Scrabble piece
34. Life story, for short

Puzzle 7.05
Sudoku

	5	9	4			1	8	7
4			3		8			1
1								4
	1		5		7		6	
	8		2	3	4		5	
	4		8		6		3	
8								6
5			6		3			9
	6	1	7		9	2	8	

Puzzle 7.06
Sudoku

	6		7	1	5		2	
			2		4			
7			3	8	9			5
2			5	4	1			8
		9		3		5		
1			9	2	8			6
5			1	9	2			7
			4		3			
	9		8	5	6		3	

Puzzle 7.07
Word Search

AARDVARK
BADGER
CAMEL
CAT
CHEETAH
CHINCHILLA
CHIPMUNK
COCKATIEL
DEER
DOG
DOLPHIN
ELEPHANT
FOX
GAZELLE
GECKO
GERBIL
GOAT
GUINEA PIG
HAMSTER
HIPPOPOTAMUS
HYENA
JAGUAR
KITTEN
LEOPARD
LIZARD
LLAMA
MONGOOSE
MOUSE
PARROT
PEDIGREE
PIG
PONY

PORCUPINE
PORPOISE
PUPPY
RABBIT
RACCOON
RAT
REPTILE
RHINOCEROS
SKUNK
SNAKE
TIGER
WALRUS
ZEBRA

```
L H G J W E S U O M J T Q L Q V S M M M
N H P N Y X L O T D C E N I P U C R O P
X L E P E D I G R E E I A E M E P D N K
P L P V N F C A C E S Q L A L O P B G Z
W U P K E Q P T K K C I T D R I T F O X
P R A C C O O N U U B O O A O D T I O P
C H F U E R G N C R P E N P N L V P S S
S I Y L R D K I E O K M C I R D P A E V
E O C A T T C G P A C H O P H O Y H R R
D Q P Q I N H P N A R K Z K W R P U I K
I E N G A A I S D E E A A G E C K O G N
A Y E X O H N Y B A T N B T L H T D T U
U R Y R J P C F A P S T I B I E W A L M
J A Y A T E H B D R M W I U I E A G I P
J A M T C L I L G X A E Z K G T L R H I
D C G A Z E L L E O H M L I Z A R D N H
T W M U L T L K R Y D A N E Y H U G E C
X E R N A L A E N C Z X B I D G S R B L
L A O I F R B O Z P U R N R U V J U X H
M D L H D B P M G A A X H Q G L B N Z J
```

Puzzle 7.08
Double Scramble

Cheesy Snack

NYRAG   _____

OIBRT   _____

UHOGC   _____

FNIYT   _____

HYOEN   _____

_____

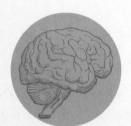

Cut Back on Brain Drains

Based on research, there might be a connection between high levels of soda drinking and memory problems, so it may be a smart idea to cut back on your intake. There is also evidence in animal models that shows that higher levels of soda intake are associated with faster aging.

Puzzle 7.09
Provider

3 LETTERS

AYE	INS
DEB	MED
DYE	NAY
END	NEB
EWE	SKI
EYE	WAS
HAD	WAY

4 LETTERS

ABRI	KANE
ALMA	LAGS
ANTI	LUNK
BANE	LYRE
BRAD	MESH
BRAE	NEON
CHAD	OPES
CLOD	PECS
DEAL	PENS
DEER	RAND
ELHI	RANT
EYRE	REIN
GROG	ROMP
HERO	SLIP
IDES	SOLI
ILEA	SOPS
IRED	STUD
IRKS	WREN

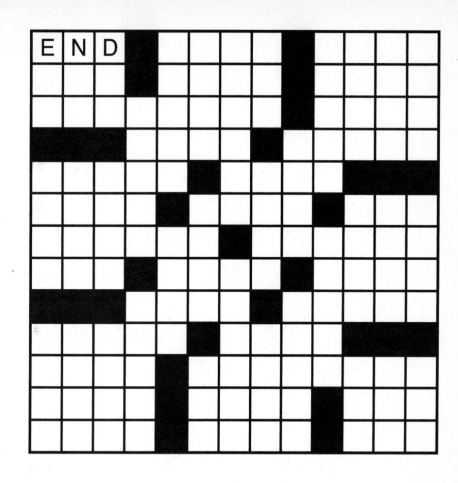

5 LETTERS

ABBES	HEEDS
ARRAS	MICAS
CODAS	SEEDS
CODES	SEWED
DRAIN	SLOGS

6 LETTERS

COSTAR	SEANCE
GIGOLO	TIPTOE

8 LETTERS

EYEDROPS
WOODSMAN

Puzzle 7.10
Cryptoquote

VZA OFECGVNWV VZOWJ OT WCV VC TVCE

KDATVOCWOWJ. YDGOCTOVH ZNT OVT CLW GANTCW

SCG AIOTVOWJ.

—NUMAGV AOWTVAOW

Hint: The word "curiosity" is found in the quote.

Puzzle 7.11
Cryptoquote

Z XHKK HK Z NVPQNI AWHGX EQKHSCQE TI

CZAOWQ AV KAVB KBQQGR JRQC JVWEK TQGVUQ

KOBQWLNOVOK.

—HCSWHE TQWSUZC

Hint: The word "lovely" is found in the quote.

Puzzle 7.12
Crossword

Across

1. Narcotic
6. Leave out
8. Alias letters
9. Neptune's domain
10. FedEx alternative
11. She sheep
14. Nebraska city
16. The yoke's on them
18. Chinese Chairman
20. Director's cry
24. Clearasil target
25. Home to Denali National Park
26. Intended
28. Massage with the hands
30. Spartan
32. Cheshire Cat feature
33. Singer Tucker
34. Chow down
35. Blender setting to reduce to mush
36. Fairy tale starter
37. Pay-___-view

Down

2. Baseball is our national one
3. Eisenhower nickname
4. Motorists' org.
5. Outfit

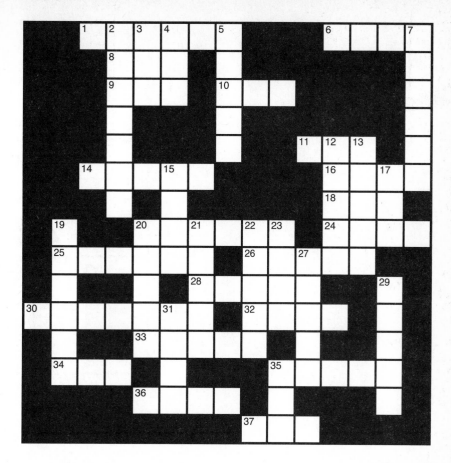

7. Bar
12. John Lennon hit
13. Precise
15. Bumpkin
17. Long, long time
19. River in a Strauss waltz
20. Liability's opposite
21. Spoken for
22. Alpha's opposite
23. At hand
27. French farewell
29. Went out with
31. Parade spoiler
35. "The Raven" poet

Puzzle 7.13
Sudoku

1		8				3		6
			5	3	2			
	3		6		8		7	
	1	3	4	7	6	2	8	
		2				7		
	7	4	3	2	5	6	9	
	8		9		4		6	
			2	6	7			
4		5				9		7

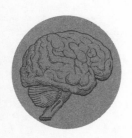

Learn a Foreign Language

Being multilingual is extremely beneficial these days, and learning a foreign language can also be quite mentally challenging because it requires the thoughtful assimilation of new information and a strong memory. Struggle with those verbs, pore over grammatical structure, force yourself to speak it at every opportunity, and stick with it even when it seems futile. Learning a new language is often a long-term commitment (years or more) despite what many popular programs state, so you might not get the hang out it right away. The minute it feels like your brain is stretching, though, you're already succeeding. Once you've learned a new language, reward yourself with a vacation to a country where the language is spoken so that you can practice speaking the new language and learn more about the country's culture.

Puzzle 7.14
Double Scramble

Musical Toy

ERODR   _____

IKKHA   _____

RBAOT   _____

EBZAR   _____

OUCRC   _____

_____

Puzzle 7.15
Double Scramble

Little One

DCEYA   _____

ELDOG   _____

ICGRA   _____

HADNY   _____

SEUIS   _____

_____

Puzzle 7.16
Sudoku

6	4	7	9				3	
		9						
3	2			1	6	4		
7						3		5
	5	3				6	1	
4		1						7
		5	2	6			4	3
						5		
	7				9	8	6	2

Puzzle 7.17
Sudoku

4				3	8	1		5
8		9	7		1			
3					6			
1	4				7			9
	7						3	
5			3				7	1
			4					6
			1		3	9		2
6		4	8	9				3

Puzzle 7.18
Forget Me Not

nut

potato

hospital

daughter

sail

father

basket

paste

milk

spoon

Puzzle 7.18
Forget Me Not

_____   _____

_____   _____

_____   _____

_____   _____

_____   _____

What Was Your Time?

If you decided to challenge yourself further and time your puzzling session, be sure to write down your results below. Take a moment to reflect on your past sessions and acknowledge any improvements made along the way. With every chapter in this book, you should be able to notice how much more focused and alert your brain is becoming.

_____

_____

_____

_____

_____

_____

_____

_____

_____

_____

_____

_____

_____

_____

_____

_____

_____

CHAPTER 8

MEMORY LEVEL

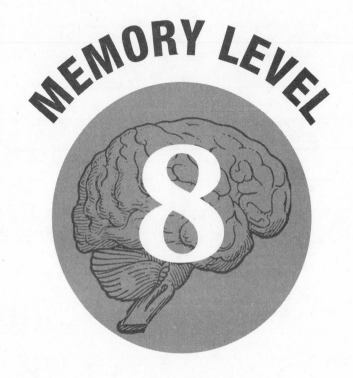

Puzzle 8.01
Forget Me Not

bulb

feather

air

copper

ink

sign

root

ticket

soap

moon

Puzzle 8.01
Forget Me Not

_____ _____

_____ _____

_____ _____

_____ _____

_____ _____

Puzzle 8.02
Provider

3 LETTERS

AAH   ILK
AAS   IRK
ARS   MAS
AWN   MHO
CEL   MOC
COW   NIL
DUE   ODS
DUI   OIL
ELM   OVA
GHI   REB
GOA   TAS
HAM   VIA
HAS   WHA

4 LETTERS

AIDE   OGRE
ARFS   OLLA
ASKS   OSSA
AVOW   PAVE
CLUE   RAIL
COCA   RAPS
COLA   SACS
DAWN   SAGO
FLOE   SAIL
GEES   SATE
HARE   SHED
HEEL   SIBS
HIES   SKIT
ISLE   SLED
LACE   TAMS

TANS   WHEE
TWOS   WHIT
USES   WRAP

5 LETTERS

CADET
COTES
GREET
SALES
SOLOS
SPACE
STOWS
TRIER

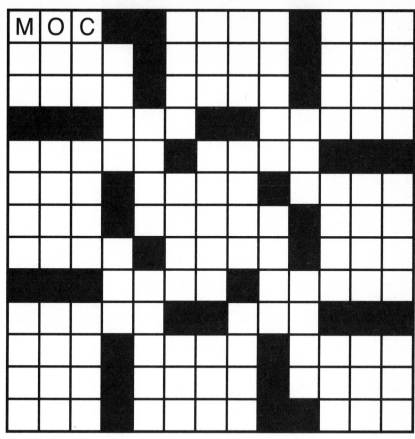

Puzzle 8.03
Cryptoquote

AQ ECHU UPLC MPI ZHQF FSC PFSCE NCEYPQ'Y
WPPK. AQ EPTHQFAG UPLC MPI ZHQF FSC PFSCE
NCEYPQ.

—THEWHECF HQKCEYPQ

Hint: The word "romantic" is found in the quote.

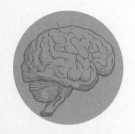

Have Sex Often

Sex stimulates your entire brain. During orgasm, blood flows through your brain, creating that fabulous sense of release and gratification. Orgasms also stimulate deep emotional parts of the brain and thus provide a calming influence. A healthy sex life leads to greater overall satisfaction and better overall functioning, which leads to a healthier person. This also leads to better memory and concentration over time.

Puzzle 8.04

Crossword

Across

1. Part of UCLA
4. It'll keep you warm in the winter
7. Actress Thurman
9. Low in fat
10. "If all ___ fails . . ."
11. Vaughan of jazz
13. Back talk
15. Em, to Dorothy
16. Something to lend or bend
17. ___ firma
19. An amoeba has one
20. ___ Gras
22. Bar order, with "the"
23. Cheney's predecessor
24. Crock
26. On the ball
28. "___ to Joy"
29. Debtor's letters
30. Hoover, for one
32. Pageant crown
34. ___ spumante
35. Hanker for

Down

2. ___ Na Na
3. Kick off
5. Guarantee
6. Run through
7. Gorbachev's nation
8. ___ culpa
9. Detest
12. Not digital
14. Practice boxing
15. St. Louis landmark
18. ___ colada
20. Syrup flavor
21. Burn balm
22. WWW address
25. Prefix with cycle or focal
26. Fess up
27. "Mazel ___!"
28. Quaker ___
31. Mayberry boy
33. Lend a hand

Puzzle 8.05
Sudoku

	4	5	8	3	1	6	9	
	6	3		2			7	5
2				7				4
			2	6	5			
		6				8		
			1	8	4			
3				1				7
	7	1		4		5	8	
	8	4	6	5	7	2	1	

Puzzle 8.06
Sudoku

	8			1			5	
	6	5		9		4	7	
		9	5	6	2	8		
5		7				6		1
		4		3		2		
9		8				7		5
		2	1	4	9	3		
	4	6		5		1	8	
	9			7			2	

Puzzle 8.07
Word Search

BAHT
BOLIVARES
DEUTSCHE MARKS
DINARS
DIRHAMS
DOLLARS
DRACHMAE
ESCUDOS
EURO
FORINT
FRANCS
GUILDERS
KORUNY
KRONER
KWACHA
LEI
LEVA
LIRE
MARKKAA
NEW SHEKELS
PESETAS
PESOS
POUNDS
RAND
REAIS
RINGGITS
RIYALS
RUBLES
RUPEES
RUPIAHS
SCHILLINGS
YEN
ZLOTYCH

```
T S H A I P U R U B E S I X P O Y S Q O
D G K R G U S Y K O X O X E A H C A W K
Y S S R U M B F S L Z J S R A N I D G P
K C K X A P R N F I I E L S A T O B Q N
C F L H R M E E H V T L R R I Y A L S N
R L R Q S S E E T A Y I F I L Y T A E A
E I S R B B U H S R R S J A L H Y W P G
D X N C U S S M C E Y S I Q Z V S Q O V
G B I G J J F G N S W M W A A H U J U V
U E K F G L U O N D T J I Y E N A M N B
Q R T T N I R O F I M U K K E R V C D X
W M Y W L K T G D J L D E N O I E F S H
I M L D B H N S G O Q L A D S A L O B P
S A E L A Z F V U Y S K I E M S D F S F
H R T B F A W P A Y L J U H O U V B A A
S K A E H U N S N S H R C H C Y T O L Z
P K B L X H O U H O O A J S K S K H Y F
H A X A L W R A N D R S E L B U R Q W N
Z A N B M O U B E D S Z E Y U V F W P X
A R P J K Q D Y R U E E I P H W A F Q I
```

Puzzle 8.08
Double Scramble

Drink Slowly

TSART   _____

ILFRE   _____

EECNI   _____

RRERO   _____

CUTUN   _____

_____

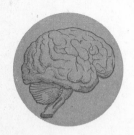

Play the Name Game

Enhance your memorization at every opportunity and take advantage of the challenges life presents every day. For example, at social events, or whenever introduced
to someone new, repeat the person's name to yourself three times and then use it in
conversation. Meet as many people as possible, and then test yourself the next morning to see how many you can remember. Give yourself bonus points for remembering
how they were dressed or what they did for a living.

Puzzle 8.09
Provider

3 LETTERS

ALE	LOO
ARB	ORA
ARE	PAD
ARK	PEA
ART	PIE
CON	RET
DES	RIA
EAT	SEA
IRE	SER
KAY	STY
KIT	TAR
LEE	TOT

4 LETTERS

ACME	MANY
ALAE	MATT
ALOE	MOTH
ALPS	OLEO
ALTS	PANS
APSE	RATS
ARCS	RIOT
ARIA	ROOT
ARTS	SEES
BANS	SELL
CASE	SERA
COAT	SOUP
COKE	STYE
FLAT	TETS
HELP	TOLU
LOAN	TOTE

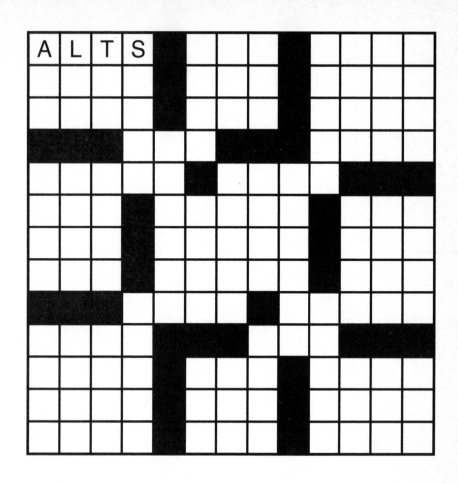

5 LETTERS

AFORE	MASTS
ARRAS	PLOTS
CAMEL	SALSA
COOLS	STELE
MASSE	TENSE

6 LETTERS

ELAPSE	SESAME

Puzzle 8.10
Cryptoquote

WPOE UNV BZZW QV YZ BQTMSSIAOS UAQN

PFHZTBAQE PTZ NPDDE; WPOE, PWAF STZPQ

PCCIMZOJZ, PTZ MQQZTIE WABZTPYIZ.

— QPJAQMB

Hint: The word "struggling" is found in the quote.

Puzzle 8.11
Cryptoquote

ZJNYWF IBCX C QCG KRYZ IBYG BY LZ DCJPBX

RTT BLZ PJCNK LZ XBY UYZX YOLKYGDY CZ XR

IBCX ZRNX RT QCG BY LZ.

— D.Z. WYILZ

Hint: The word "evidence" is found in the quote.

Puzzle 8.12
Crossword

Across

3. Townshend of The Who
5. Gun rights org.
7. Penned
9. Activities on eBay
11. Answer to a charge
12. Came to
13. False god
15. Edison's middle name
18. Took a load off
20. Composer Copland
22. Mrs. Bush
24. Broom ___ (comics witch)
26. Former Russian space station
27. Shake up
31. Tune out
33. HI Hi
36. Feline line
37. Resistance to change
38. Dig like a pig
39. Tied

Down

1. Mexicali Miss
2. Sister of Venus Williams
3. Tempo
4. Astronaut Grissom
5. It might be found in a ring
6. Govern
8. Mojavi Desert AFB
10. Places for prices
14. Lord's Prayer start
16. Place to hibernate
17. Actor Kilmer
19. Assert without proof
21. Inauguration Day recital
23. Actress Jolie
24. She was named after Mt. Everest climber?
25. Historical period
28. Peru's capital
29. Stranded motorist's need
30. The Buckeye State
32. Memo
34. Prefix with lock or knock
35. ___ Lanka

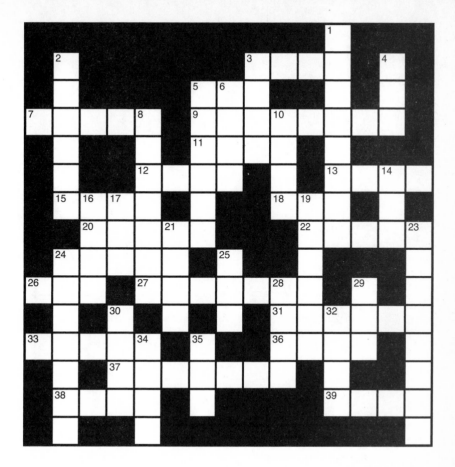

Puzzle 8.13
Sudoku

	1		9	3	4		5	
	8						4	
9				5				1
1	6	5				4	3	7
		7	4	1	5	6		
4	2	8				5	1	9
6				4				2
	7						6	
	3		7	9	6		8	

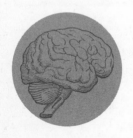

Eat Breakfast

Breakfast is one of the most important meals, yet it is probably the most frequently skipped meal of the day. The word "breakfast" describes exactly what it does: breaks a fast. After a good night's rest, your body has gone eight to twelve hours without food or energy. Blood sugar, or glucose, which comes from the breakdown of food in the body, is your body's main source of energy. Eating food provides your body with a fresh supply of blood glucose, or energy. The brain in particular needs a fresh supply of glucose each day because that is its main source of energy. (The brain does not store glucose.) Eating breakfast is associated with being more productive and efficient in the morning hours. Breakfast eaters tend to experience better concentration, problem-solving ability, strength, and endurance. Your muscles also rely on a fresh supply of blood glucose for physical activity throughout the day.

Puzzle 8.14
Double Scramble

Unifying Idea

HTEIF   _____

ECLTE   _____

ITXES   _____

NIORM   _____

LLOEH   _____

_____

Puzzle 8.15
Double Scramble

Place for Books

BHAIT   _____

LGAEE   _____

YFNCA   _____

STMEA   _____

ALROB   _____

_____

Puzzle 8.16
Sudoku

		4	2	9			6	
						2		
9		7	1					4
		3		2	4		1	5
4	7						2	3
6	1		5	3		4		
7					1	9		2
	9							
	4			8	9	5		

Puzzle 8.17
Sudoku

7	5		9		1	2		
9	8			5		4	1	
1				8				6
		7					4	5
5	1					2		
2				4				1
	4	9		1			8	2
	3		7		2		5	4

space island

ornament orange

coat church

brain heart

edge ring

Puzzle 8.18
Forget Me Not

_____   _____

_____   _____

_____   _____

_____   _____

_____   _____

What Was Your Time?

If you decided to challenge yourself further and time your puzzling session, be sure to write down your results below. Take a moment to reflect on your past sessions and acknowledge any improvements made along the way. With every chapter in this book, you should be able to notice how much more focused and alert your brain is becoming.

_____

_____

_____

_____

_____

_____

_____

_____

_____

_____

_____

_____

_____

_____

_____

CHAPTER 9

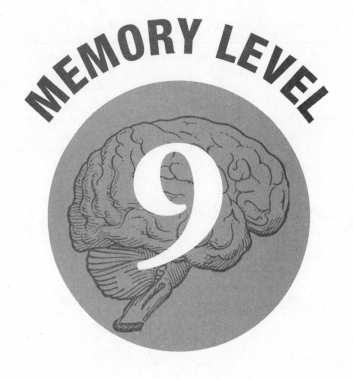

MEMORY LEVEL

Puzzle 9.01
Forget Me Not

family   prison

engine   goat

garden   wire

watch   cloud

foot   rice

Puzzle 9.01
Forget Me Not

_____   _____

_____   _____

_____   _____

_____   _____

Puzzle 9.02
Provider

3 LETTERS

ALA	MOA
ANT	NAE
ARS	ORT
AVE	PAP
AYE	PUT
BOY	RAP
DAD	SAT
ERA	SET
ERN	TEN
GAT	TOM
GEN	TSK
MAY	

4 LETTERS

AGEE	RARE
ALEE	ROUT
AMPS	SALE
APED	SASS
APES	SATE
ASPS	SCAT
BARE	SEAS
BRAD	SERE
EYES	SLOE
LAVA	SLOG
NENE	SOLO
ONES	SPAT
PATS	STAB
PELE	TEED
PLEA	TENS
POLL	TOIL
PSST	TORE

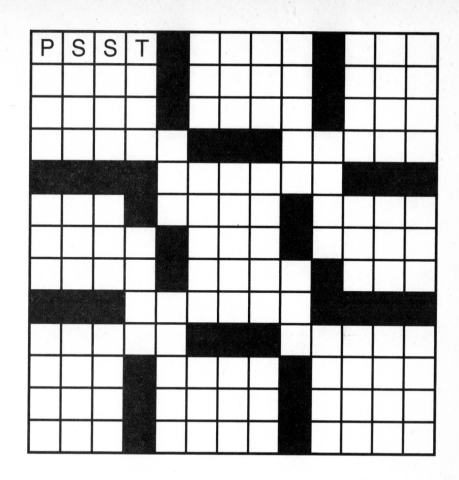

5 LETTERS

ALTAR	ROAST
BLAST	SEEDS
ESSES	STABS
KAPPA	STEED
MINCE	

6 LETTERS

ARMADA
ASTERS

Puzzle 9.03
Cryptoquote

TQ HXBE ID XODQ TQJBZUQ OR HOLQU AIZ RMQ

JMBGJQ RI XILQ, RI YINC, RI FXBA, BGE RI XIIC

ZF BR RMQ URBNU.

— MQGNA LBG EACQ

Hint: The word "chance" is found in the quote.

Limit High-Fat Foods

Improperly stored oils and fats will go rancid, and that's just what happens in the body when you eat a high-fat diet. Since the brain and nervous system are very high in fat, some researchers take the idea of rancid fat one step further and speculate that rancid fat may be damaging the brain by causing free radicals (unstable molecules that potentially cause cell damage). A high-fat diet increases a person's risk of getting Alzheimer's, and some studies, such as one that was published by Professor Daniel Michaelson in *Journal of Neuroscience*, have even found that the risk is increased when both the APOE4 gene and a high-fat diet are present.

Puzzle 9.04
Crossword

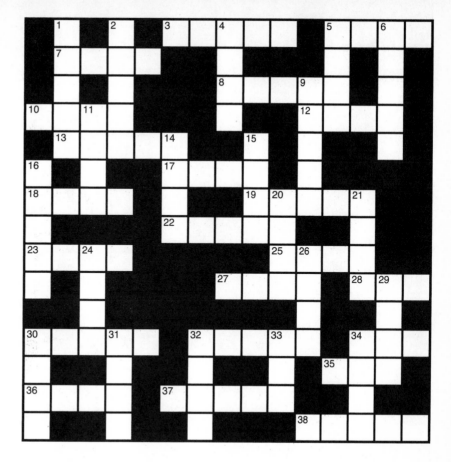

Across

3. Gawk
5. Gratis
7. Horn sound
8. Funeral song
10. Bona ___
12. Stink
13. Mea ___
17. Threesome
18. Luau dance
19. In the know
22. ___ Carlo
23. Mary Kay competitor
25. Swiss peaks
27. Nothing more than
28. Preschooler
30. Fritter away
32. Bluegrass instrument
34. Gymnast's goal
35. Relatives
36. Graph line
37. Entice
38. V-formation fliers

Down

1. Room at the top
2. Monopoly buy
4. Artist Warhol
5. Run away
6. Conjure up
9. Actress Garbo
11. Twofold
14. Molecule part
15. Paint layer
16. Bundle or arrows
20. Put on
21. Sunrise direction
24. Paddles
26. Letterman rival
29. Warning sign
30. Withdraw gradually
31. To-do list item
32. "___ there, done that"
33. Stick (out)
34. "Newsweek" alternative

Puzzle 9.05
Sudoku

5	9	6	2	1	7	3	8	4
			4		9			
		4				2		
4	6						2	8
	5	2				1	4	
8	1						5	3
		5				4		
			6		8			
7	4	3	1	9	5	8	6	2

Puzzle 9.06
Sudoku

	1		8	7	3		4	
9			1		2			
5	8					7		
				3			6	4
6								9
4	3			9				
		4					8	6
			6		7			3
	6		3	4	1		7	

Puzzle 9.07
Word Search

ALAN JAY LERNER
ART BLAKELY
ART TATUM
ARTIE SHAW
BARBER
BARRY GIBB
BEETHOVEN
BERLIOZ
BRAHMS
BRUCKNER
CAROLE KING
CHARLIE PARKER
CHICK COREA
CHOPIN
COLE PORTER
COUNT BASIE
DAVE BRUBECK
DAVE STAMPER
DIZZY GILLESPIE
HERBIE HANCOCK
HOLST
IRVING BERLIN
JOHNNY MERCER
KENNY CLARKE
LESTER YOUNG
LIONEL HAMPTON
LISZT
LOUIS ARMSTRONG
MENDELSSOHN
ORNETTE COLEMAN
OSCAR HAMMERSTEIN
PUCCINI

SCARLATTI
SCHUBERT
SHOSTAKOVICH
STEPHEN SONDHEIM
THELONIOUS MONK
WYNTON MARSALIS

```
S H O S T A K O V I C H O P I N D C M A
M A C S S M W Y N T O N M A R S A L I S
U S O S C A R L A T T I L E E N V N C G
T D U R H A J E S O E A K Z T Y E O A N
A A N E U Q R L V K N R B M R L B T R U
T V T C B O O H R J A O R I O E R P O O
T E B R E H I A A P H T A E P K U M L Y
R S A E R W L Y E M Z T H H E A B A E R
A T S M T C L I B S M E M D L L E H K E
E A I Y Y E L E I C R E S N O B C L I T
R M E N R R R L D B T U R O C T K E N S
O P N N A L O U I S A R M S T R O N G E
C E E H I B E E T H O V E N T A U O I L
K R C O W A H S E I T R A E T E S I N C
C N Z J B A R R Y G I B B H Z M I L I B
I R V I N G B E R L I N V P E E Q N C A
H P R C D I Z Z Y G I L L E S P I E C R
C B O A N A M E L O C E T T E N R O U B
Y C W X T H E L O N I O U S M O N K P E
K N H O S S L E D N E M B R U C K N E R
```

Puzzle 9.08
Double Scramble

Close Encounter

HCTHA   _____

USAUL   _____

GNERI   _____

LABGE   _____

SUCAE   _____

_____

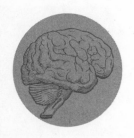

Learn Five New Words Each Day

Like the athlete who takes time to warm up and flex his or her muscles before engaging in a strenuous activity, flexing your brain cells with a few basic word-play exercises warms up your mental engine. Words are fun; they expand your mind. Pick up your dictionary and pick out five words you don't know. Commit their definitions to memory and write five sentences using them in different ways. See if you can recite their definitions from memory the next day. And then learn five more. If you're not in the habit of using your mind to memorize poetry, song lyrics, obscure facts, or unfamiliar names, acquiring new vocabulary can be a challenge. However, "practice makes perfect," and as you persevere, you'll soon discover that the task of committing words to memory will become increasingly easier to achieve and more satisfying.

Puzzle 9.09
Provider

3 LETTERS

AGA   OAT
ANA   ODS
BRA   ORE
DOS   PAS
GAS   POI
HES   RIG
MAD   SAG
MOB   TAT
MOP   TOE
NOR   YEA

4 LETTERS

AEON   OSES
AERO   OTTO
AGIO   OWED
AMAH   SEGO
ARID   SETA
CARD   SNAG
DEAL   SODS
DRAT   TARS
ELSE   TEEN
EPEE   THAT
ERGS   TOMS
EVES   TOPE
HERO   TRIM
HITS   TSAR
MAGS   TYNE
OARS   WOES

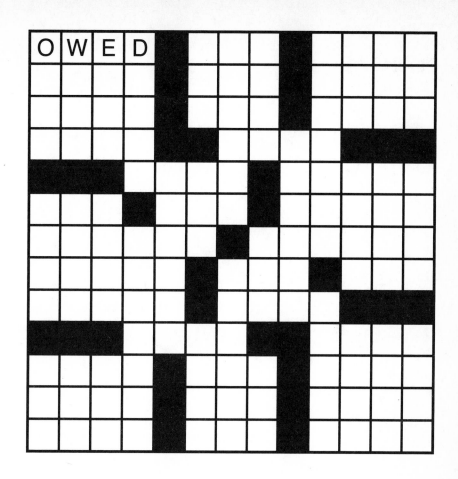

5 Letters

DENSE   STATS
RAGES   STOAT
RAVEN   TRESS

6 LETTERS

ARENAS   ROASTS
ARREST   STREET
PESETA   THRONE

7 LETTERS

CAMERAS   NEATENS

Puzzle 9.10
Cryptoquote

CRS NIX YRV FVSU XVC QSIF DVVF LVVOU RIU

XV IFJIXCIDS VJSQ CRS NIX YRV BIXXVC QSIF

CRSN.

—NIQO CYIHX

Hint: The word "books" is found in the quote.

Puzzle 9.11
Cryptoquote

OXUXUKXO RSFFQCXNN EWXNC'Z EXFXCE DFWC

LRW VWD SOX WO LRSZ VWD RSTX; QZ EXFXCEN

NWIXIV WC LRSZ VWD ZRQCM.

—ESIX ASOCXHQX

Hint: The word "solely" is found in the quote.

Puzzle 9.12
Crossword

Across

3. Cherry seed
6. Playwright David
8. "No bid," in bridge
11. Jump on one foot
12. Singers Hall and ___
13. Dots in the ocean
16. Clothing
18. Traveler's reference
19. Move in the breeze
21. Sept. preceder
22. Not in class
26. Americans, to Brits
28. Appraiser
30. ET's transport
32. Skirt bottoms
33. Screwdriver, e.g.
36. Deuce beaters
38. After-Christmas event
39. Rank above cpl.
42. "Now it's clear"
43. Barnyard clucker
44. Venus de___
46. Caruso or Domingo
47. Not wide

Down

1. Love, to Pavarotti
2. Game show host Sajak
3. Hushed "Hey you!"
4. Spicy Asian cuisine
5. Rapid
7. Lean slightly
8. Letter before kappa
9. Doesn't fail
10. Close, as an envelope
14. Noticed
15. Isle of exile for Napoleon
17. Helpers for profs
20. Capone and Pacino
21. Major League brothers' name
23. Roof support
24. No, to Nikita
25. Picture card
27. Curly cabbages
28. Chapter and ___
29. Future attorney's exam: abbr.
31. Like Rapunzel's hair
34. Astronomical hunter
35. Deplete, with "up"
37. Calendar periods
40. Chew
41. On, as a lamp
43. Billy Joel's "Tell ___ About It"
45. Martial arts expert Bruce

Puzzle 9.13
Sudoku

		8	4		9		7	
4	1							
3					8			
5				3			2	1
9				4				5
2	6			8				9
			3					4
							5	7
	5		7		1	3		

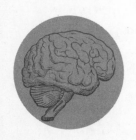

Keep a Journal

Keeping a daily journal will inspire you to think about your life, patterns in your life, what you're really thinking, etc. Formulating thoughts and writing them down will benefit your brain in multiple ways, particularly if you strive for complexity, expand your vocabulary, or become more observant. It will also help relieve stress, especially if you dispel your worries onto the page and truly release them.

Puzzle 9.14
Double Scramble

Gold or Silver

ALWFU   _____

SRMAH   _____

TSNEE   _____

TLEAR   _____

EGPTY   _____

Puzzle 9.15
Double Scramble

Sweetheart

DMLAE   _____

GEALL   _____

GAONL   _____

EQALU   _____

TNOFR   _____

Puzzle 9.16
Sudoku

4	5	7	1	9				
1							6	
					2			5
5	7		4		9		2	
	2			1			4	
	9		2		3		8	1
2			3					
	3							8
			7	1		2	9	3

Puzzle 9.17
Sudoku

	9	6	2		7	5	4	
7		5				1		2
5	2		8		9		1	6
8	1		5		4		2	9
4		8				3		1
	5	2	3		8	9	6	

thread

mouth

flag

secretary

match

test

bee

fruit

wind

girl

Puzzle 9.18
Forget Me Not

_____   _____

_____   _____

_____   _____

_____   _____

_____   _____

What Was Your Time?

If you decided to challenge yourself further and time your puzzling session, be sure to write down your results below. Take a moment to reflect on your past sessions and acknowledge any improvements made along the way. With every chapter in this book, you should be able to notice how much more focused and alert your brain is becoming.

_____

_____

_____

_____

_____

_____

_____

_____

_____

_____

_____

_____

_____

_____

_____

CHAPTER 10

MEMORY LEVEL

10

Puzzle 10.01
Forget Me Not

eye	pencil
square	hand
curve	station
stick	land
shelf	berry

Puzzle 10.01

Forget Me Not

_____   _____

_____   _____

_____   _____

_____   _____

_____   _____

Puzzle 10.02
Provider

3 LETTERS

ACT	LAT
AGE	LIE
AGO	MAT
AHA	MIL
ALS	NUN
ASP	OBI
ATE	RAS
BAM	RES
COO	ROD
EON	SEN
HOP	SHY
LAB	SPY
LAS	TAS

4 LETTERS

ABLE	LEER
ACHE	LOCI
AGAR	LOOT
AGUE	MANE
ALBS	METE
ANTE	MOPE
APER	OAST
ARBS	ODES
BRAE	RACE
BRAG	RATE
BRAS	ROTE
BROS	SANS
CORE	SASH
GLEE	SEAL
KEEL	SEMI

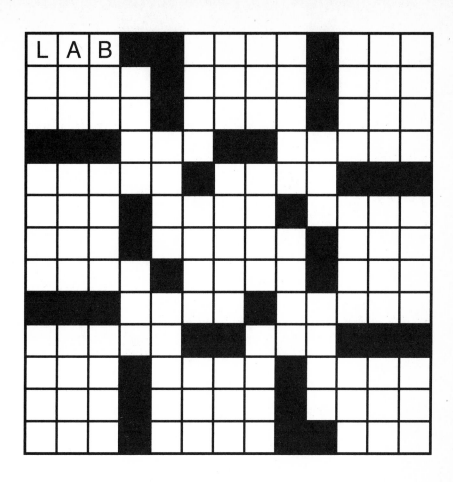

SOAK	TEND
SOMA	THEE
SOTS	VISE

5 LETTERS

GATOR	SATES
GESTE	SAVER
MATES	SLATS
PSALM	TREED

Puzzle 10.03

Cryptoquote

JKS MKX'L QIL LK HAKKEI AKG JKS'TI QKPXQ LK

MPI. KT GAIX. JKS HUX KXFJ MIHPMI AKG JKS'TI

QKPXQ LK FPZI. XKG.

— RKUX WUIC

Hint: The word "decide" is found in the quote.

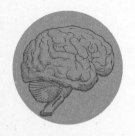

Join a Book Club

This has a triple bonus. Most book clubs pick challenging books and set a specific deadline for reading them. Part of the fun is analyzing a book's structure, theme, characterizations, plot, and other concepts that may not be familiar to you, but this process will also be mentally challenging. Additionally, groups typically gather for discussions, offering you opportunities to socialize, engage in meaningful conversation, and invigorate yourself.

Puzzle 10.04

Crossword

Across

1. Roasts' hosts
4. Storytelling uncle of fiction
7. Electric power network
8. House extension
10. Bear's abode
12. One who mimics
15. Sufficient
16. Gala gathering
18. Place for a keystone
20. French holy woman: abbr.
21. Has some success
23. Far-flying seabird
26. "Nightline" host Koppel
27. ___ Kett of old comics
30. ___ support (computer help)
32. Makeshift shelter
33. Average mark
35. Basketball hoop
36. Notes after mis
37. Title for Churchill
38. ___ room (play area)
39. Paul who sang "Puppy Love"
40. Road topper

Down

1. Ron of "Tarzan"
2. Stockholm's country

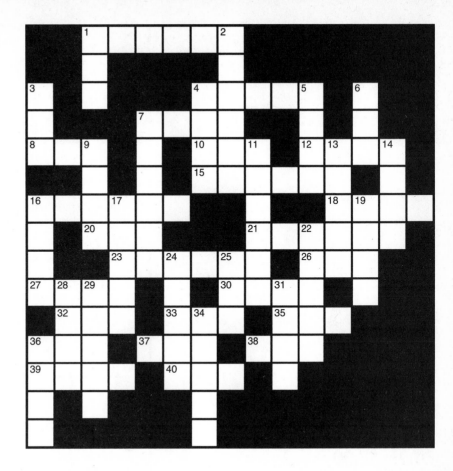

3. Metal in rocks
4. Theme park attraction
5. Hosiery problem
6. Deuce, in tennis
7. Trimmed beard
9. Soap-making substances
11. Piece of pasta
13. Terrible twos, for one
14. Boulder
16. Duffer's cry
17. March 17 honoree, for short
19. Went by taxi
22. Guiding philosophy

24. Silently understood
25. Summer: Fr.
28. Holier-___-thou
29. Walrus features
31. Ship's staff
34. Clear the chalkboard
36. Raise crops

Puzzle 10.05
Sudoku

3		4						5
			7	2		9		
							1	
1			8				5	6
	5			1			2	
7	8				2			4
	4							
		1		7	3			
2						3		9

Puzzle 10.06
Sudoku

8		5	2	1				6
	3		6			8		
		1						
				9	4	3		
		8				6		
		4	5	7				
						7		
		3			7		8	
7				6	1	4		9

Puzzle 10.07
Word Search

ABIGAIL
AIDAN
ALEXANDRA
ALEXIS
ALYSSA
ANDREW
ANGEL
ANNA
BENJAMIN
BROOKE
CALEB
CHLOE
CONNOR
DESTINY
ELIJAH
ELIZABETH
EMMA
GRACE
HANNAH
HUNTER
ISABELLA
ISAIAH
JACK
JENNIFER
JOHN
JORDAN
JULIA
KATHERINE
KAYLA
MADISON
MATTHEW
MICHAEL

NATALIE
NICHOLAS
NOAH
PAIGE
RYAN
SAMANTHA
SAMUEL
SARAH
SAVANNAH
STEPHANIE
TAYLOR
THOMAS
ZACHARY

```
P X D F U Z H S B R D W U P Y X B R L E
U M S Z V P A I G E E E B R O O K E Y L
C B J N W M T N T F Z R N A D I A T Q B
G H Z J U Z A S U I V D L D D D H L N M M
F A Z E E T K N B N S N I T C D Y U R B
I B L J B R B G G N Y A V I C M S H C A
V E V E I N A H P E T S M O J M S A N S
V M L J X S B C P J L B N A X K A L E Z
X A E Q K A T H E R I N E E N N N L M A
C T W N S V N H H A O N L N R T I E M C
U T H O M A S D B R X I M C J J H B A H
J Z N N M N Z I R M Z C P Z A A X A Q A
T S C A Y N G Q K A D H V H W Z M S J R
H A G T F A I C B D G O C D E S T I N Y
M T Y A I H H E N I V L Y Z H T L X N J
A F N L R L T A N S Z A G B T Q K E U E
Z N H I O H D X N O O S R U T C L L N B
A F O E Y R P U U N K H A I A S I A E K
C C J H O D K A Y L A O C J M A Y E H D
N G X J I K T S A R A H E F C R W Q F O
```

Puzzle 10.08
Double Scramble

One of the Senses

SEARE   _____

OMRYA   _____

ELESA   _____

DNUOS   _____

VLREE   _____

_____

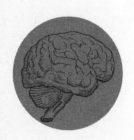

Stay Hydrated

Simple dehydration can cause the brain to react in strange ways. Fogginess, dizziness, and lack of concentration are all symptoms of dehydration. Water is one of the most abundant substances in your body and is what your body needs in the greatest amounts. Almost 55–75 percent of an adult's body weight is water. Water is present in every part of your body: It comprises 83 percent of blood, 73 percent of muscle, 25 percent of body fat, and even 22 percent of bones. Water plays a vital role in almost every major function in the body. Water helps regulate body temperature through perspiration. It transports nutrients and oxygen through the body, carries waste products away from the body cells, cushions joints, and protects body organs.

Puzzle 10.09
Provider

3 LETTERS

ALL	MED
ANE	MEN
BAY	OCA
BOO	OHO
ELD	OLE
ERS	PAL
HAY	SON
HON	SPA
HUH	TAE
ICE	TAN
LAG	WIN
LET	

4 LETTERS

ABET	OLDS
AGED	PREP
ALAS	ROAN
ALIT	ROSE
ANSA	SAIL
AURA	SCAD
BOWS	SEAT
CORN	SHAD
DICE	SHES
ELLS	SHMO
EPOS	SHOO
ERAS	SLAM
GOBS	SLED
LAIN	SONS
LANE	SYNE
MADE	TAEL

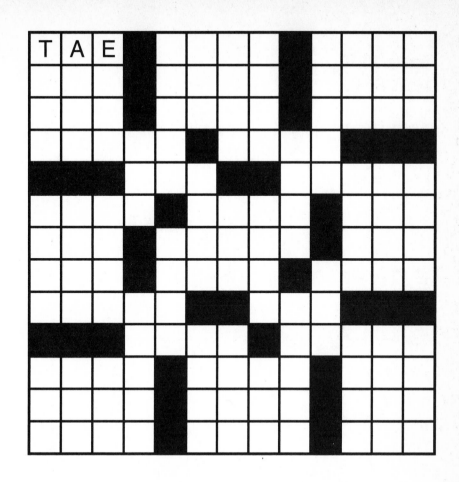

TAPA	TOON
THEM	TRIO
TOLE	YENS

5 LETTERS

ANGST	RESTS
ASSES	SLATE
BESTS	SNARE
PANED	TASSE
PICOT	

Puzzle 10.10
Cryptoquote

WNP ZFWWZP TODPEPEGPDPI RLWV CH MFOIPVV

ROI ZCAP RDP WNP GPVW KRDWV CH R

KPDVCO'V ZFHP.

— QFZZFRE QCDIVQCDWN

Hint: The word "kindness" is found in the quote.

Puzzle 10.11
Cryptoquote

GIF JFTFBW IFFJY UCIL GWVFXY, CIJ YG WVF

PVGEF VGQYF BY SQBEW BI WVF CBX CIJ UQYW

YGGI TGUF WG WVF NXGQIJ.

— SCEWCYCX NXCTBCI

Hint: The word "house" is found in the quote.

Puzzle 10.12
Crossword

Across

1. Southwest Indian
4. Soprano Callas
9. Devious plot
11. Sir, in Seville
12. Shootout time, maybe
13. Justice ___ Day O'Connor
15. Women in habits
16. Addition result
17. Net material
19. Moslem cleric
21. 4:00 social
22. Part of UV
24. Self-absorbed
26. Ventilates, with "out"
29. English cathedral city
30. "What ___ become of me?"
31. Store, as grain
32. Wall Street index, with "the"
34. Movie awards
36. Headline
37. Canceled, as a launch

Down

2. Missouri mountains
3. Wader with a curved bill
5. The "A" in DNA
6. Clean again
7. Restaurant list
8. Hope and Barker
10. Tooth protector
11. Dad, to Grandpa
14. Tattle on
18. Roof's edge
19. Garden flowers
20. Retail store
21. Every now and ___
22. A choir may sing in it
23. Clothes alterer
25. Boxing site
27. Scotch mixer
28. Six o'clock broadcast
33. Not a duplicate: abbr.
35. Not pro

Puzzle 10.13
Sudoku

6					1			8
			4					
4	1				7		2	
5			8	6	2			3
				4				
2			3	7	9			6
	7		6				5	4
					8			
3			9					2

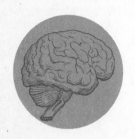

Dance, Dance, Dance

We all know that music and dance stimulate us in many ways. The rhythmic beats, melodies, and flowing physical movements all stimulate the senses and the brain. The parietal lobes are associated with sensation, visual-spatial functions, attention to objects in space, and other functions. Music tends to stimulate areas associated with reflection, autobiographical memories, and creativity, and can have some therapeutic effects on individuals. All areas of the brain are affected positively by rhythmic movements that involve balance and coordination. So choose songs that have moved you in the past or that elicited joyful, playful, or romantic feelings.

Puzzle 10.14
Double Scramble

String Quartet Member

JTEEC   _____

NROWE   _____

EGELD   _____

ECVAR   _____

ACLHT   _____

_____

Puzzle 10.15
Double Scramble

Elaborate Meal

HETET   _____

AFRVO   _____

AOCNR   _____

YSTOR   _____

AXTER   _____

_____

Puzzle 10.16
Sudoku

9	7		2		8		4	5
4			5		1			9
3		9	4		5	6		8
7		5	6		3	1		4
6			8		4			2
1	4		9		7		5	6

Puzzle 10.17
Sudoku

3			7	4		8		
								5
8		6		3	5	7	2	1
	5						9		4
6								2
9		4					7	
7	8	9	6	2		5		3
5								
		3		5	8			7

ear	cork
mountain	rod
card	ice
ship	wood
insect	rain

Puzzle 10.18
Forget Me Not

_____   _____

_____   _____

_____   _____

_____   _____

_____   _____

What Was Your Time?

If you decided to challenge yourself further and time your puzzling session, be sure to write down your results below. Take a moment to reflect on your past sessions and acknowledge any improvements made along the way. With every chapter in this book, you should be able to notice how much more focused and alert your brain is becoming.

_____

_____

_____

_____

_____

_____

_____

_____

_____

_____

_____

_____

_____

_____

_____

_____

CHAPTER 11

MEMORY LEVEL

11

Puzzle 11.01
Forget Me Not

money   gun

parcel   step

glove   cushion

story   pen

sock   soup

Puzzle 11.01
Forget Me Not

_____   _____

_____   _____

_____   _____

_____   _____

_____   _____

Puzzle 11.02
Provider

3 LETTERS

AAH	OPS
AMP	OPT
ARM	PAR
ASS	PEE
BEE	ROB
BOA	ROT
EEL	SEE
ELS	TAO
EMS	TEE
ERE	THE
HAE	TIS
ION	WET
LEA	

4 LETTERS

ABRI	OATS
ALMA	OLES
ANTS	OPES
AREA	OPTS
ASEA	PEEP
BARN	PHAT
CELL	PROA
ETHS	PSIS
HEAT	RENT
IOTA	SABE
LAMP	SARI
LAPS	SEAM
LASE	SEAR
LASS	SEER
LOAM	SEPT

SETS	TONE
SIRE	TOOL
SOON	TORA
TENT	TWAS

5 LETTERS

ALINE	STARS
CASAS	START
MATTE	TESTS
SPARS	

Puzzle 11.03
Cryptoquote

RNJY BIGRM HY NWJNWNUYRQ SDOONYF NJ BY

TIGRM IWRQ HY HIFW DU USY DLY IJ YNLSUQ

DWM LFDMGDRRQ DOOFIDTS YNLSUYYW.

— CDFP UBDNW

Hint: The word "eighty" is found in the quote.

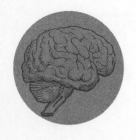

Get Plenty of Rest

Prolonged fatigue prevents the mind and body from functioning at optimal levels, depresses the immune system, and wears down the entire system—physical, mental, and emotional. Deep and genuine rest is transformative in many ways. Being in a state of true rest connects us to our intuitive levels and the innate pattern of health and well-being residing within. Sleep allows the brain to juggle the input of new information to produce flashes of creative insight. It's fairly common to wake from a power nap with an "aha" moment. In other words, get plenty of rest—it's good for your brain!

Puzzle 11.04
Crossword

Across

1. Loewe's Broadway partner
2. Kid's question
4. Open with a key
7. Took a photo of
10. Hard-boiled item
12. West Coast wine valley
13. 50/50 share
15. Go on a buying spree
16. ___ and vinegar
17. Cow's hurdle, in rhyme
18. Tell a fib
19. Water absorber
22. ___ and true
26. Find a sum
27. Lighten, as a burden
30. Scarlett's spouse
32. Part of the eye
33. State west of Mont.
34. Pepsi or RC
35. Put on weight
38. Loses brightness
39. ___ bender (minor accident)
41. "___ and the Wolf"
42. Sing in the Alps

Down

1. Enjoy a joke
2. Hornet, e.g.
3. Plant's beginning
5. Go ___ a tangent
6. Mounds
8. Hightail it
9. ___ clef
11. Bodega owner
14. On ship
20. Unseal
21. Auto repair shop
22. Jobs to do
23. Driver's lic. and such
24. Translate, in a way
25. Part of PST: abbr.
28. "You've got mail" addressee
29. Spanish ladies: abbr.
31. Having prongs
34. Tabby
36. At ___ rate
37. Altar vows
38. FBI agent
40. Minister: abbr.

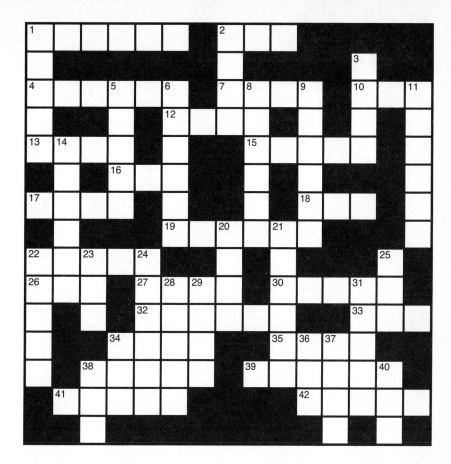

Puzzle 11.05
Sudoku

8	5		9		4			
							8	7
4							9	3
	4			6			7	
6			7		3			4
	3			5		9		
9	1							6
5	6							
			6		8		5	2

Puzzle 11.06
Sudoku

4	2	5	7			6		
6								
	3	7		2				
1	7			9	3			5
5								8
2			1	8			3	6
				7		8	6	
								4
		4			8	5	1	2

Puzzle 11.07
Word Search

AVIATION
BACKPACK
BALL
BASEBALL
BASKETBALL
BEACH
BIKING
BIRDING
BOATING
CAMPING
CANOEING
CANTEEN
CLIMBING
CYCLING
EQUESTRIAN
FISHING
GOLF
HIKING
HUNTING
KAYAKING
MOUNTAINS
NATURE
OCEAN
PICNIC
PLAYGROUND
RAFTING
RIVERS
RUNNING
SAILING
SCUBA
SKIING
SNOW

SPORTS
TENNIS
TRAILS
WALKING
WILDERNESS

```
C Y P F L T W S R E V I R R G Q F X H T
T E N N I S G T L Q B B L U P N B G U T
V L D A N J P N J U G B L L H J I N S U
D G E O T G W O N E A K A V I A T I O N
P H S J M U N Q B S C Y B H M F C E K W
U E S S O F R I K T G N E I L L Y O L S
U I E L U F V E K R P Z S K I O X N S J
U X N D N L T C O I B H A M D G J A L E
N K R A T B G U U A H X B B G H N C I D
Y N E C A X N E C N G I M G N I L I A S
G C D L I D I K A G N I D R I B L N R N
O N L S N D P L U G I P V J H J D C T O
K J I K S A M H D G K W R N S Z C I R W
V S W K C Q A Z U W I D E A I E S P A I
E V O K A F C R B N B E A R F A Q E E X
V W X B Y Y G E B M T A C Q S T R O P S
H B S J B O A T I N G I W A L K I N G A
F Z A B U C S K A G N I N N U R R N M Z
T Y G L H C Y C L I N G H G G L O R G R
P D U M L Z F O P L E I Z C C A W Y V S
```

Puzzle 11.08
Double Scramble

Newsstand

KKCNO _____

URBCS _____

NIKEF _____

SEOEB _____

IHSRI _____

_____

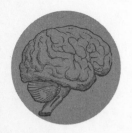

Eat Blueberries

Some foods are better for you than others. The key is to eat a diverse diet, with an emphasis on those foods with nutritional punch. Blueberries, in particular, help protect the brain and may reduce the effects of Alzheimer's disease and other forms of dementia. They have also been known to improve motor skills and learning capacity. Doctors recommend adding one cup of blueberries to your daily diet to reap their benefits.

Puzzle 11.09
Provider

3 LETTERS

AMA	OWE
AMI	RED
AWE	REF
BEG	SIT
DAB	TAM
DOR	TED
MAN	TIN

4 LETTERS

AGER	NAVE
AKIN	ORES
ALAN	ORLE
ALAR	PANE
AMID	PENS
CAKE	SAVE
CLAY	SCUP
CREW	SLOT
EARN	SONE
ELAN	SURE
FLEE	TAPS
GAME	TERN
HERE	THRU
IDES	TOWS
LOOS	TROP
LOPE	TUBE
LUNA	UNIT
MANO	WANE

5 LETTERS

ACRES	MASON
AWARE	SPATS
CRESS	STETS
CRONE	STILE
ECRUS	TONES

6 LETTERS

ENISLE	OBEYER
LETHAL	PSEUDO

8 LETTERS

REGAINED
RHEOSTAT

Puzzle 11.10
Cryptoquote

VXCXJ AWJJZ DYWTU UKX ESMX WR ZWTJ

QKJSEUBDE UJXX. SV UKX XZXE WR QKSILJXV,

UKXZ DJX DII UKSJUZ RXXU UDII.

—IDJJZ ASILX

Hint: The word "children" is found in the quote.

Puzzle 11.11
Cryptoquote

AKO KBDKONA ZNO HU MRVBARC BN QHA AH

FRPO FHTO FHQOW, XZA AH FRPO FHQOW IH

FHTO UHT AKO XOAAOTFOQA HU CBUO.

—KOQTW UHTI

Hint: The word "capital" is found in the quote.

Puzzle 11.12
Crossword

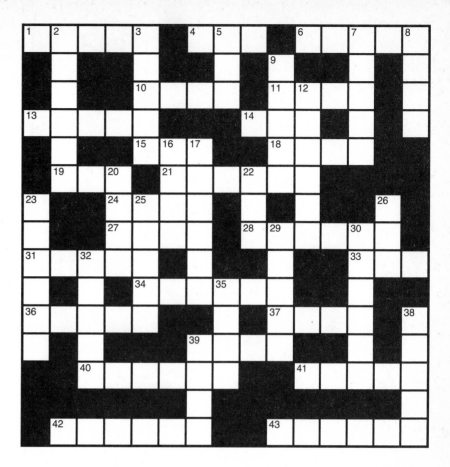

Across

1. Ignore the script
4. Bit of wordplay
6. Acquire knowledge
10. Give a longing look
11. Salon colorings
13. Krispy Kreme product
14. Weed digger
15. Engine additive letters
18. Raisin ___ (cereal)
19. Fri. follower
21. Confidential matter
24. Former Fed chief Greenspan
27. Left, at sea
28. Teeter-totter
31. Bronco-riding event
33. Restroom, informally
34. Element in salt
36. Dad's brother
37. Oxen coupler
39. Sothern and Jillian
40. Escalator alternative
41. Movie star's rep
42. Democratic Party symbol
43. Pitching great Tom

Down

2. Sags
3. Winter footwear
5. One: Fr.
7. Fire-setting crime
8. Scent detector
9. Hacienda material
12. Seuss turtle
16. Pre-1917 Russian ruler
17. Group of five
20. Record on video
22. Streets: Abbr.
23. Open courtyard
25. In need of tightening
26. Bygone airline
29. Television awards
30. Declare in court
32. Conduits
35. Rustic lodgings
38. Broadway performer
39. Pretentiously showy

Puzzle 11.13
Sudoku

8	3	9	4			7	5	
	2				3			
1			7	6				
						2		
	3			5		1		
	6							
				3	4			1
			9				8	
	7	5			8	3	9	2

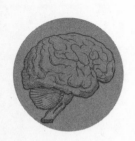

Learn to Play a Musical Instrument

According to Daniel G. Amen, author of *Making a Good Brain Great*, students with experience in musical performance scored 51 points higher on the verbal part of the SAT and 39 points higher on the math section than the national average. Learning to play an instrument has been associated with better study habits, better discipline, and an ability to complete tasks in other studies as well. It can also be helpful in developing and activating the entire brain and is likely to improve brain function overall.

Puzzle 11.14
Double Scramble

Problem for Jonah

LERAS   _____

TBAOU   _____

GWEDE   _____

RTENE   _____

YDARH   _____

_____

Puzzle 11.15
Double Scramble

Full of Good Cheer

EOMDL   _____

BTOOR   _____

YILDE   _____

OARST   _____

EALYR   _____

_____

Puzzle 11.16
Sudoku

6	4	2			9	7	3	
	5			6			4	
9			5			6		2
8	6							
			9					
							5	8
1		5			4			3
	8			5			9	
	9	6	2			5	8	1

Puzzle 11.17
Sudoku

6		5	3		8	7		2
1		2				8		9
2	4		9		1		5	3
3	5		6		7		8	4
5		4				3		8
7		1	4		6	9		5

wheel	bird
plate	bottle
neck	train
kettle	pocket
heart	key

Puzzle 11.18
Forget Me Not

_____   _____

_____   _____

_____   _____

_____   _____

_____   _____

What Was Your Time?

If you decided to challenge yourself further and time your puzzling session, be sure to write down your results below. Take a moment to reflect on your past sessions and acknowledge any improvements made along the way. With every chapter in this book, you should be able to notice how much more focused and alert your brain is becoming.

_____

_____

_____

_____

_____

_____

_____

_____

_____

_____

_____

_____

_____

_____

_____

_____

_____

_____

CHAPTER 12

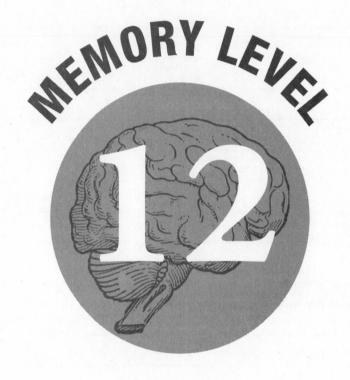

MEMORY LEVEL 12

Puzzle 12.01
Forget Me Not

worm   stick

hat   fish

head   band

shelf   leg

hook   nut

Puzzle 12.01
Forget Me Not

_____ _____

_____ _____

_____ _____

_____ _____

_____ _____

Puzzle 12.02
Provider

3 LETTERS

APE
ARC
BEN
BUY
COS
DOM
EYE
FIB
FLU
FRO
LAW
LUV

OOH
RAH
SAW
SRI
THO
TOY
WAD
WAG
WEB
WOO
YES

4 LETTERS

ACES
AMIE
ARES
ARFS
AWED
AWLS
AYES
COVE
GENE
HOES
HOOT
LACE
MILS
MORT
OHMS
OMIT
OOPS

PAPA
PARA
PFFT
REST
RILE
ROUE
SETT
SHOW
SILO
SLAT
SLAW
SORE
STAR
STET
TARE
TEST
TODS

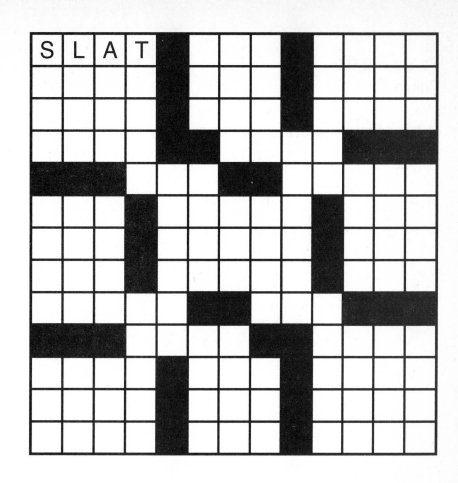

5 LETTERS

BROOD
IMAMS
MOCHA
POSTS
REAPS

RESEE
SEEPY
SPATE
TESTY

6 LETTERS

EMBRYO
TRADER

Puzzle 12.03
Cryptoquote

UALCJWKM WU QDAF AYAJMKDWFH WU UAKKPAG.

QDAF FXKDWFH LEF DEVVAF KX MXC. UALCJWKM

WU KDA GAFWEP XN PWNA.

—HAJSEWFA HJAAJ

Hint: The word "settled" is found in the quote.

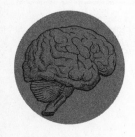

Limit Caffeine

One of the world's most popular drugs, caffeine is a stimulant that affects the central nervous system, the digestive tract, and metabolism. Caffeine is found in coffee beans, tea leaves, cocoa beans, and products derived from these sources. It is absorbed quickly in the body and can raise blood pressure, heart rate, and brain serotonin levels (low levels of serotonin cause drowsiness). Withdrawal from caffeine can cause headaches and drowsiness. The pharmacological active dose of caffeine is defined as 200 milligrams, and the daily recommended not-to-exceed intake level is the equivalent of one to three cups of coffee per day (139 to 417 milligrams). The stimulant properties of caffeine can interfere with getting sufficient sleep important for proper brain functioning. However, at low doses, caffeine can also increase mental functions, so just make sure it's consumed in moderation.

Puzzle 12.04
Crossword

Across

2. Coffee-break time
4. Drive or reverse
5. Geometric figure with equal angles
6. Hole for a lace
9. Yeses at sea
12. Letters after els
14. Plaza Hotel heroine
15. ___ Way galaxy
17. Winter precipitation
18. "You can ___ horse to . . ."
20. Gives a thumbs-up
21. Dentists' tools
24. Spelling or Burr
26. Roam (about)
27. Radio interference
29. Letter carriers' grp.
30. Hospital area: abbr.
31. South Dakota's capital
32. Disappoint, with "down"
33. Encl. with a manuscript
34. Have a bite

Down

1. Roll-call call
2. Not false
3. Cairo's waterway
7. Have a chat
8. Luau garland
10. Duncan toys
11. Georgia and Ukraine, once: abbr.
13. Stag party attendees
14. Airline that serves only kosher food
15. Month after Feb.
16. Dolts
17. Get all sudsy
19. Prepares for publication
22. Transparent plastic
23. Adjusts to fit
25. Leaf collectors
26. Charles de ___
27. Mideast canal
28. Tarzan's raisers

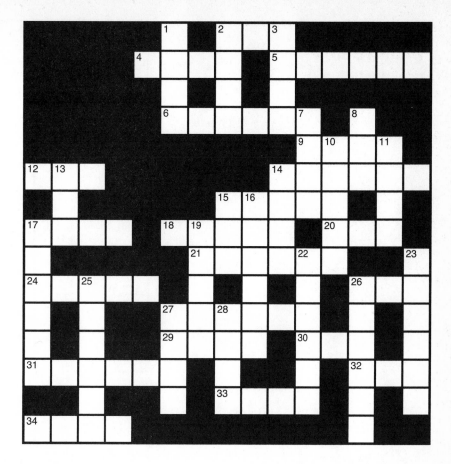

Puzzle 12.05
Sudoku

			7					9
	9			2	3	6		1
	5						4	
	8		3	9	1			
1								3
			4	8	7		5	
	3						9	
6		1	8	7		4		
4				6				

Puzzle 12.06
Sudoku

	7		3			5	9	
	5	9	8		1			2
		3						
			4			3		
		6		1		8		
		5			7			
						2		
6			5			8	9	7
	1	4			3		5	

Puzzle 12.07

Word Search

ARCHERY
ATHLETICS
AUTO RACING
BADMINTON
BASEBALL
BASKETBALL
BOATING
BOWLING
BOXING
CHEERLEADING
CRICKET
CROSS COUNTRY
CURLING
CYCLING
DANCE
DARTS
EQUESTRIAN
FENCING
FISHING
FOOTBALL
GOLF
GYMNASTICS
HOCKEY
HORSE RACING
JUDO
LACROSSE
MARTIAL ARTS
OUTDOORS
ROWING
RUGBY
RUNNING
SAILING

SHOOTING
SKATING
SKIING
SOCCER
SOFTBALL
SQUASH
SWIMMING
TABLE TENNIS
TENNIS
TRACK
TRIATHLON
VOLLEYBALL
WRESTLING

```
C Q L L L A B Y E L L O V W N W O J G U
F U G L A G J A T H L E T I C S S U Y F
H O R N A O E S S O R C A L O T L D M O
T T O L I B O J U K B A D M I N T O N R
S E S T I C E X D F E N C I N G T C A Q
K N K U B N A S M A R T I A L A R T S I
A N I C X A G R A J A W B N E O A L T D
T I I E I I L O E B M Z P A S V C Z I V
I S N F R R U L L S D S L S L D K E C K
N G G E B T C E T F R Y C V M L J S S I
G W N U D S T M A U T O R A C I N G C A
N S D O R E C C O S U P H S A U Q S Y E
I Y O A N U H Y G N I L T S E R W G C F
H R R N M Q R F T R I A T H L O N N L R
S J I C H E E R L E A D I N G I A I I W
I S K C H S Y E K C O H Z L T D F N N A
F V M C J V G N I L W O B O A T I N G H
D A R T S T O Z G N I X O B Y B G U R A
S A I L I N G D C M P H G N I W O R S J
F P S L L A B T F O S W I M M I N G N R
```

Puzzle 12.08
Double Scramble

Pitchfork Wielder

LAEEV   _____

RYNOI   _____

RVSEE   _____

TRYID   _____

ELEPO   _____

_____

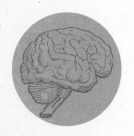

Curb Your Stress

Reduce the amount of stress and anxiety in your life. Stress is one of the most common causes of transient insomnia; it keeps the brain awake and functioning long into the night or wee hours of the morning. Stress and worry can interfere with sleep. Acknowledging the problem is the first step, followed by a resolution to take care of those problems you can and a promise not to dwell on those you can't. Learning relaxation techniques, such as breathing exercises and meditation, can also help alleviate the effects of stress and worry. Excessive stress creates tension and anxiety and can lead to a variety of health problems that are not obviously linked to tension. Stress can also complicate pre-existing conditions.

Puzzle 12.09
Provider

3 LETTERS

AAS	IDS
ABA	ILL
ALP	LAM
AND	LEI
CAP	NOT
ELK	OAR
EWE	OVA
FOE	PSI
GOD	SHA
HAS	SHE
HIE	VIA
HOE	

4 LETTERS

AFAR	LOSS
AIDE	MALE
ALES	MITE
ALLS	NEAT
ALSO	PATE
AVOW	PEPS
BRIT	PEST
BYTE	POLE
CHIS	READ
CONE	RUES
DIME	SAKE
EAVE	SEIS
GREW	SHAG
HOBO	SKIP
ILIA	SOPS
IRES	SPAS

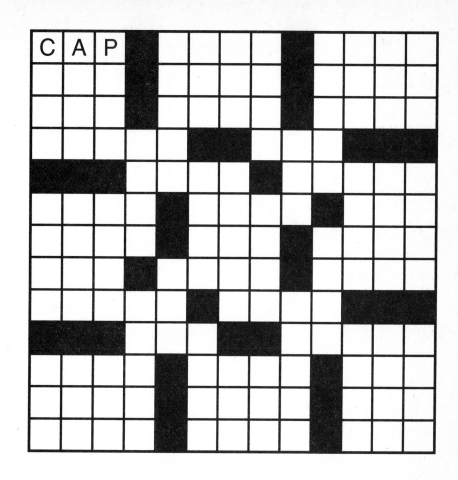

STOA	TELE
SWAT	TOGS
TEES	YULE

5 LETTERS

ADAPT	SHRED
AREAS	SOAKS
PASEO	TASTE
RECAP	TEETH
SETAE	

Puzzle 12.10
Cryptoquote

UX MTAOT JM PYGGOOA, RMYT AOPUTO ZMT

PYGGOPP PIMYNA FO DTOHJOT JIHX RMYT ZOHT

MZ ZHUNYTO.

— FUNN GMPFR

Hint: The word "greater" is found in the quote.

Puzzle 12.11
Cryptoquote

FLWJW ZY DAF WDANTL BGJEDWYY ZD GRR FLW

XAJRB FA VNF ANF FLW RZTLF AS WUWD ADW

YOGRR PGDBRW.

— JAHWJF GRBWD

Hint: The word "world" is found in the quote.

Puzzle 12.12
Crossword

Across

1. Certain test results
5. Groups of troublemakers
7. ___ nous (between us)
8. Long sandwich
9. Lacking skill
12. Gobi or Mojave
13. Whooping birds
16. Actress Sarandon
17. Accused's excuse
19. Eugene's state
21. Pre-election event
22. Comical Laurel
25. "Leaving ___ Vegas"
27. Building annexes
29. Brother of Prince Charles
30. Where the Reds and the Browns play
31. Kasparov's game
32. On an ocean liner

Down

2. "A Streetcar Named Desire" woman
3. Calcutta's home
4. Lacking moisture
5. Golden-egg layer
6. Santa's vehicle
7. Stops fasting
10. Leaf through
11. Actor Hume

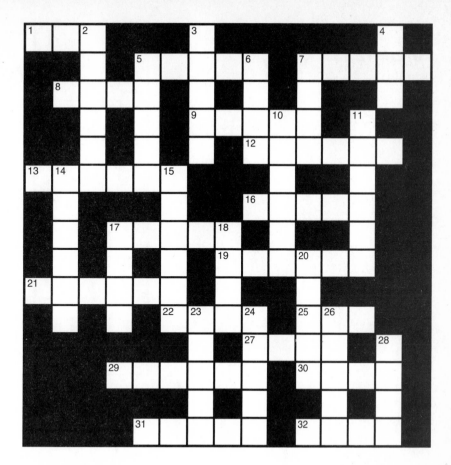

14. Fixes Junior's laces
15. Treats with malice
17. "Stronger than dirt" sloganeer
18. Des Moines is its capital
20. Winemaker Ernest or Julio
23. Stooges count
24. Brilliantly colored salamanders
26. Fireplace remnants
28. Lotus position discipline

Puzzle 12.13
Sudoku

		4		3	7			
	2		9	4			1	
	6					7		4
5								
		9	6		5	2		
								1
9		5					8	
	7			5	1			2
			4	8		1		

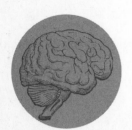

Avoid Clichés

"Cliché" is the French word for "stereotype." In other words, it's something that is worn out through repetitive use. In English, "cliché" is used to describe phrases and expressions that have crept into the language to such an extent that they have lost their freshness and original meaning. Clichés are boring and trite, yet we continue to parrot them, scarcely aware of how they clutter our speech. "Saved by the bell" is an example of a cliché. Relying on cliché is lazy. Exercise your brain by challenging yourself to avoid clichés and coming up with fresh metaphors or original expressions. And maybe you'll create a new cliché that lazy people can use when they talk.

Puzzle 12.14
Double Scramble

Symbol of Authority

OLENA   _____

QEUPI   _____

EBGNI   _____

ODLLY   _____

GOESO   _____

_____

Puzzle 12.15
Double Scramble

Military Bigwigs

IESZE   _____

RSBUT   _____

CETSN   _____

NGRAE   _____

RNOPA   _____

_____

Puzzle 12.16
Sudoku

9		3				5	7	
							1	
2	6				7			9
	3		7	8				
8	7		1	5	6		2	3
			4	3		5		
5			6				3	1
	9							
	8	6				7		5

Puzzle 12.17
Sudoku

8		6	5		4	9		2
2	3						6	5
	9						4	
5		7	2		1	8		3
9		8	7		3	6		4
	7						8	
6	8						2	1
4		2	1		8	3		9

Puzzle 12.18
Forget Me Not

arch	dust
room	cat
powder	fork
stomach	board
gold	glass

Puzzle 12.18
Forget Me Not

_____   _____

_____   _____

_____   _____

_____   _____

_____   _____

What Was Your Time?

If you decided to challenge yourself further and time your puzzling session, be sure to write down your results below. Take a moment to reflect on your past sessions and acknowledge any improvements made along the way. With every chapter in this book, you should be able to notice how much more focused and alert your brain is becoming.

_____

_____

_____

_____

_____

_____

_____

_____

_____

_____

_____

_____

_____

_____

_____

_____

_____

_____

CHAPTER 13

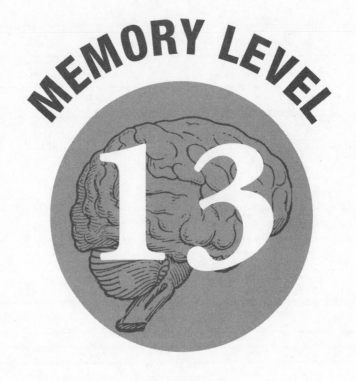

MEMORY LEVEL 13

knife	cart
record	stocking
poison	drink
curtain	fire
bird	boat

Puzzle 13.01
Forget Me Not

_____   _____

_____   _____

_____   _____

_____   _____

_____   _____

Puzzle 13.02
Provider

3 LETTERS

ACE	OHM
ANI	ONE
APT	ORS
AWL	OSE
BAA	PAX
CUM	REP
DOE	RHO
FAS	RUN
GOT	SAE
INN	SOS
KOI	TAP
LOP	

4 LETTERS

ACRE	HARE
ADDS	HAST
AGON	LOCA
ANEW	LOUT
ANNA	MASS
APEX	MORE
ARCO	OBOE
AWOL	OUTS
BAKE	PASS
BANE	PLAT
BORE	PROS
DADA	RETE
DEAN	ROPE
ELMS	SALT
FOIL	SENT
FRAT	SHUN
SLAP	SOME
SLIM	STEW
SNIP	TUNA

5 LETTERS

ALONE	SHAMS
BASED	SLASH
LATHE	TESTA
LEFTS	TREES
SCOLD	

Puzzle 13.03
Cryptoquote

FICPEB AIBSAUSK PW O RSBPEEPEB. QSSNPEB

AIBSAUSK PW NKIBKSWW. ZIKQPEB AIBSAUSK PW

WXFFSWW.

—USEKG VIKH

Hint: The word "progress" is found in the quote.

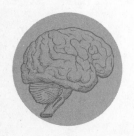

Think Positively

According to Daniel G. Amen, MD, author of *Making a Good Brain Great*, every thought releases brain chemicals. Positive, happy, hopeful, optimistic, joyful thoughts produce chemicals that create a sense of well-being and help your brain function at peak capacity; unhappy, miserable, negative, dark thoughts have the opposite effect, effectively slowing down your brain and even creating depression. If you tend to focus on what can go wrong, or what is wrong, or how unhappy you are, or how someone hurt you, these negative thoughts can dim your brain's capacity to function. It saps the brain of its positive forcefulness. Dr. Amen suggests writing out negative thoughts to dispel their power over your brain.

Puzzle 13.04
Crossword

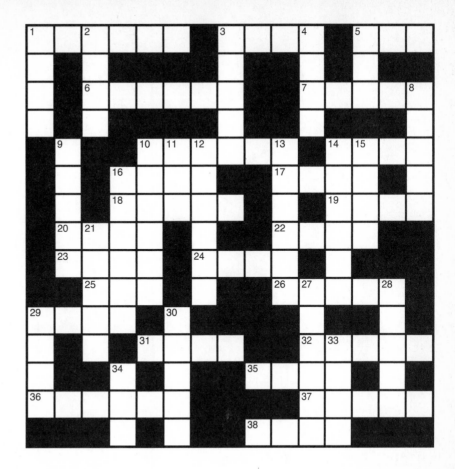

Across

1. Head over heels
3. Airshow stunt
5. G-man's employer
6. Ancient Greek city
7. Like ghost stories
10. Scented pouch
14. Boring routines
16. Rat (on)
17. Miami basketball team
18. French ___ soup
19. Three feet
20. A.k.a. Bruins
22. "Now we're in trouble!"
23. Writer of rhymes
24. Pharmaceutical
25. Suffix with lemon or lime
26. German author Hermann
29. Money in Mexico
31. ___ upon a time
32. Broadcast's sound portion
35. One named in a will
36. Pacific weather
    phenomenon
37. Prefers
38. Highlands girl

Down

1. "___ no kick from
   Champagne"
2. Be defeated
3. Dog's restraint
4. Desserts with crusts
5. Mink or sable
8. Soothed
9. Calendar girl
10. Part of Congress
11. Boxer Muhammad
12. Sun blockers
13. However
14. Synthetic fibers
15. Salt Lake state
16. Ohio port
21. Part of USCG
27. Hits the "Send" button
28. The Four Hundred
29. Tree with cones
30. ___ a happy note
33. "Mila 18" novelist
34. Three, on a sundial

Puzzle 13.05
Sudoku

5		1		6	4			
7	9			8				
8		2					3	
			5		9		6	
			1	7	6			
	2		4		8			
	1					7		5
				5			4	2
			7	4		3		6

Puzzle 13.06
Sudoku

	2				4	3	1	
	1		5	8				
9				3				
					8	1		
		4				2		
		8	9					
				4				5
				7	1		8	
	8	6	2				9	

Puzzle 13.07
Word Search

ADAMS
ARTHUR
BUCHANAN
BUSH
CARTER
CLEVELAND
CLINTON
COOLIDGE
EISENHOWER
FILLMORE
FORD
GARFIELD
GRANT
HARDING
HARRISON
HAYES
HOOVER
JACKSON
JEFFERSON
JOHNSON
KENNEDY
LINCOLN
MADISON
MCKINLEY
MONROE
NIXON
PIERCE
POLK
REAGAN
ROOSEVELT
TAFT
TAYLOR

```
L Q E Z Z L R G Y R S N O S V C R G X K
V J S R B P Z Y D G C N G W S N N P G I
H J O V O L T E K L O P O A N V E G R I
U Z R Y C O O L I D G E A S R O L Y A T
D V Q B K L U N E Y M W M H R F S H N V
N H K M E N T I R V T H K I N E I L T A
C S S Y N O J K O E E A K N A H F E I R
D U M O N S N C M J I S F G G A A F L W
E B U A E K I M L A O S O T A R P Y E D
N M Y J D C X J L H D H E O E R T K E J
N Q Z Q Y A O I I N V I N N R I F C T S
D T R C D J N C F E A A S S H S M L F I
R E V T D C K E C O A M N O O O U E D H
G F H O O V E R X A R R U B N N W V T A
K T J L Y R E L Y T R D T R U Q A E W R
C Q N N I I Y U F Z P T O K T R W L R D
S H D U P O Q Z S L J E H D G O E A M I
Q R B H W Z A U Y Q T G B U C H A N A N
R X T U L V V T C A U R E T R A C D Q G
V J Y S U W L F L W X I N O X B T P A W
```

TRUMAN
TYLER
VAN BUREN
WASHINGTON
WILSON

Puzzle 13.08
Double Scramble

Concentrate

CONEA _____

LSIEM _____

FTHIG _____

LINTU _____

ALANC _____

_____

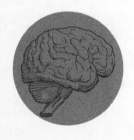

Get Free Radicals Under Control

Free radicals age your brain. A free radical is an unstable molecule that is formed when molecules within the body's cells react with oxygen. It is unstable because it has an unpaired electron that steals a stabilizing electron from another molecule, potentially causing cell damage. Antioxidants are vitamins and minerals, such as magnesium, selenium, vitamin C, and vitamin E, stored in the body whose job is to neutralize free radicals. A diet rich in these important vitamins and minerals can help minimize the effects of free radicals. If there aren't enough antioxidants available, excess free radicals begin to damage and destroy normal healthy cells, leading to degenerative diseases. They can damage any body structure by affecting proteins, enzymes, fats, and even DNA.

Puzzle 13.09
Provider

3 LETTERS

ADO   FOB
AVA   HAH
BAD   HEP
BOS   NET
DAP   ODE
EVE   PIS
FAR   TAB

4 LETTERS

ALFA   LEAN
ALMS   LEAS
AMEN   LILT
ANTA   LIMA
BEAR   MARS
CITE   MELD
CLAM   OMER
CLOD   OYER
DRAY   PEAL
DROP   PEAS
DRYS   PERT
ERRS   RIEL
ERST   ROTA
EYRE   SCAB
FEAT   SOLI
ISMS   STAY
LAMA   TATE
LAWS   VANE

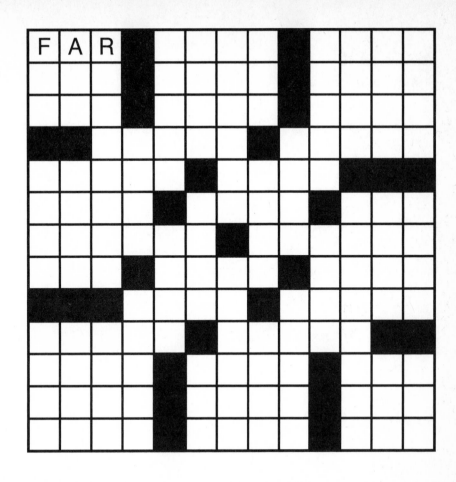

5 LETTERS

ARCED   SLAMS
AVERS   SLAPS
MODES   SOLAR
SASSY   TEENS
SETTS   TORSI

6 LETTERS

AMERCE   REDONE
ENSILE   WISEST

8 LETTERS

RESTATED
TOOLSHED

Puzzle 13.10
Cryptoquote

T PGB'X YZBX ZBJ JDF-EDB ZCGVBP ED. T YZBX

DQDCJHGPJ XG XDMM ED XID XCVXI DQDB TL TX

OGFXF XIDE XIDTC SGHF.

—FZEVDM AGMPYJB

Hint: The word "everybody" is found in the quote.

Puzzle 13.11
Cryptoquote

XK BZZ ZVUK XVYL YLK FGNKMYVUK FT GKVHI

LBQQW; FDC ZVUKE BCK BZZ RVTTKCKHY BHR

WKY YLK EBJK.

—BHHK TCBHP

Hint: The word "happy" is found in the quote.

Puzzle 13.12
Crossword

Across

1. Meal starter, often
3. "Schindler's List" star Liam
8. Eve's second son
10. Brittle cookie
12. Gloomy ___
13. Poker pot primer
15. Extends a subscription
17. Trio after R
18. Beard remover
19. Luxuriant, as vegetation
24. Goes out, as a fire
26. Spud
27. Salacious glance
28. Put up on eBay
30. Pointed a pistol
31. Hamilton bills
32. Astute
35. Put in the bank
38. Office helper: abbr.
40. Physically weak
41. "Golden touch" king
42. Bathroom hanger
43. Enjoy the taste of

Down

1. T-bone or porterhouse
2. On a liner
4. Snail-like
5. Remind too often
6. Annoyers
7. Christmas songs
9. Greyhound vehicle
11. Llama's land
14. Baseball deals
16. Sound in a cave
20. Used up, as money
21. Actress Tomei
22. Bluto's rival
23. Clears snow from
25. Actress Worth
29. Jar tops
30. Question's opposite: abbr.
33. Cattle groups
34. Ralph ___ Emerson
36. Bit of bridal attire
37. Handed out cards
39. "The Wizard of Oz" dog
41. "Oh, give ___ home . . . "

Puzzle 13.13
Sudoku

2		3	6				5	7
6	5							
1						6	3	
4			5	2				
		1	3		8	7		
				4	7			6
	3	6						8
							7	9
8	1				5	4		2

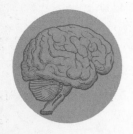

Flirt

According to Daniel G. Amen, MD, author of *Making a Good Brain Great*, when you feel an attraction to someone, areas deep in the brain, rich in the neurotransmitter dopamine, light up with pleasure. Extra dopamine courses through your body and brain, generating feelings of well-being. Your brain stem also activates, releasing phenylethylamine (PEA), which speeds the flow of information between nerve cells. "Taken together, the release of dopamine and PEA explains why, when we are around someone we feel attracted to, we feel a 'rush' and our hearts beat faster. Attraction is a powerful drug," reported Dr. Amen.

Puzzle 13.14
Double Scramble

Breakfast Sizzler

ANSAL   _____

CONEU   _____

BADER   _____

CRIAH   _____

LOALW   _____

_____

Puzzle 13.15
Double Scramble

Neck Warmer

MECAL   _____

AORZR   _____

NAAGI   _____

RAIYF   _____

SEEPL   _____

_____

Puzzle 13.16
Sudoku

4			7		2			9
5		2				7		1
		7				4	2	
		9	4					5
6	7						1	4
3					1	8		
	1	5				9		
9		6				1		7
7			1		9			6

Puzzle 13.17
Sudoku

1	5	7						6
8								
		3	6	7				5
5			1	3		4		
7		1		4		8		9
		8		9	5			1
3				1	4	6		
								4
6						3	9	8

net   hair

brick   cotton

grip   earth

hook   door

drawer   star

Puzzle 13.18
Forget Me Not

_____ _____

_____ _____

_____ _____

_____ _____

_____ _____

What Was Your Time?

If you decided to challenge yourself further and time your puzzling session, be sure to write down your results below. Take a moment to reflect on your past sessions and acknowledge any improvements made along the way. With every chapter in this book, you should be able to notice how much more focused and alert your brain is becoming.

_____

_____

_____

_____

_____

_____

_____

_____

_____

_____

_____

_____

_____

_____

_____

_____

_____

CHAPTER 14

MEMORY LEVEL 14

Puzzle 14.01
Forget Me Not

throat

foot

drawer

camera

sheep

book

knife

pencil

stem

library

Puzzle 14.01
Forget Me Not

_____   _____

_____   _____

_____   _____

_____   _____

_____   _____

Puzzle 14.02
Provider

3 LETTERS

ALB	HUE
ALT	LAC
AXE	LAD
BID	MON
BRR	NAN
CAD	OKA
EAU	ROE
EFT	SAL
EKE	SOT
EMU	SOU
HEH	SOW
HIT	TEA
HMM	WIG

4 LETTERS

ABED	EGER
ALBA	EWES
ALEF	MAID
AMAS	MAMA
ARMS	MARE
ASHY	MOUE
AWES	MUTE
AXON	NAME
BASE	ORAD
BATE	ORCA
BEST	PEND
BIKE	PESO
BLOB	REBS
BRAT	REES
DELE	ROLE

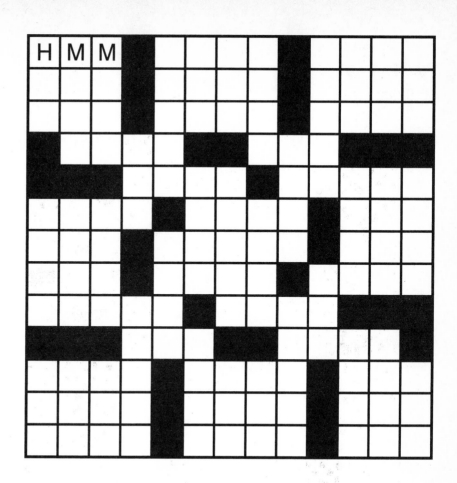

SAKI	SULK
SAND	TSKS
STAT	TUBS

5 LETTERS

ANTES	REMAP
BASER	SERAC
BASTE	SLEEP
OREAD	STYES

Puzzle 14.03
Cryptoquote

GFP UF YBR RFP, UY'L FSY YBR DRGKL UF DSNK

XUMR YBGY WSNFY. UY'L YBR XUMR UF DSNK

DRGKL.

— GEKGBGO XUFWSXF

Hint: The word "count" is found in the quote.

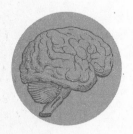

Take Magnesium

This mineral is an absolute must for proper brain function in that it aids neuron metabolism, helps reduce brain damage from ischemia (a lack of blood flow to the brain), and boosts the effectiveness of certain antioxidants. Low levels of intracellular magnesium are associated with brain cell death in Alzheimer's disease. (In healthy brains, the two minerals have a relatively equal ratio.) Every cell in the body needs magnesium. Magnesium deficiency can result from an increase in urine output—like that caused by diuretics—poorly controlled diabetes, and alcoholism. Adults over eighteen should consult their physicians before taking any dietary supplements to increase their magnesium intake.

Puzzle 14.04
Crossword

Across

1. Pizzeria fixtures
3. Mattress filling
4. 7, on a sundial
8. In high style
12. Hair-setting item
15. Comment ending
17. Ocean bottoms
19. "Sesame Street" regular
21. "___-di-dah!"
22. One who calls balls
24. Topic for Dr. Ruth
25. Back-breaking dance
26. "The Canterbury ___"
29. Knight titles
30. Shamu or Keiko
31. Suffix with north or south
33. Sedan or coupe
35. Boll eater
36. PhD exams
38. Actress May
39. Evil woman
40. Really impress

Down

1. "___ Twist"
2. Sound thinking
5. Just sitting around
6. Mental quickness
7. Accelerator or brake
9. Trunk fastener
10. Snake charmers' snakes
11. Fence openings
13. Put on the payroll again
14. Half a ticket
16. Fishing line holder
18. Med. care choices
20. Talmud language
23. Modest response to a compliment
27. Online letter
28. Leaf-gathering tool
32. Parts in plays
34. Angry feeling
36. Early afternoon hour
37. Scatter seed

Puzzle 14.05
Sudoku

				4	3	7		
3						5	6	
9		8			5			4
				1		6		
		1	8		6	2		
		5		3				
5			1			4		7
	4	6						9
		9	4	5				

Puzzle 14.06
Sudoku

1	8	7	4				2	
	5					9		
9	4							7
6			3		2			
		9				2		
			9		8			3
2							7	6
		4					8	
	7				3	5	9	2

Puzzle 14.07

Word Search

ALABAMA
ALASKA
ARIZONA
ARKANSAS
CALIFORNIA
COLORADO
CONNECTICUT
DELAWARE
FLORIDA
HAWAII
IDAHO
ILLINOIS
INDIANA
IOWA
KANSAS
KENTUCKY
LOUISIANA
MARYLAND
MASSACHUSETTS
MICHIGAN
MINNESOTA
MISSISSIPPI
MISSOURI
MONTANA
NEBRASKA
NEVADA
NEW HAMPSHIRE
NEW JERSEY
NEW MEXICO
NEW YORK
NORTH CAROLINA
NORTH DAKOTA

```
I T N A G I H C I M H A W A I I S T N W
L O K R O Y W E N S M S A X E T B N E T
O F W K P A N I L O R A C H T U O S E N
U Z L A X Y D E L A W A R E O R T A S Y
I G A N O Z I R A W S X S D T V N S S U
S M I S S O U R I H J U A H I H E N E H
I D N A L S I E D O H R C R P M B A N C
A P N S N K S U H C O A G A P A R K N M
N T C E E G T I A L R I L N I T A F E J
A E O Y W A O S O O N L N A S O S W T S
M N N K H M S C L I C L A T S K K P N F
O D N C A A E I A N A I D N I A A J E N
H P E U M D N X R R L N A O S D T O W A
A P C T P A H E I N I O V M S H O R J X
L Y T N S K A T U C F I E F I T S E E H
K E I E H S P R R J O S N X M U E G R Q
O D C K I A V F L O R I D A H O N O S U
K V U E R L I E A I N A V L Y S N N E P
V Z T R E A W A S H I N G T O N I U Y K
A L A B A M A R Y L A N D T N O M R E V
```

OHIO
OKLAHOMA
OREGON
PENNSYLVANIA
RHODE ISLAND
SOUTH CAROLINA
SOUTH DAKOTA
TENNESSEE
TEXAS
UTAH
VERMONT
WASHINGTON
WEST VIRGINIA

Puzzle 14.08
Double Scramble

Supermarket Section

LDAYE   _____

IRONB   _____

YNUOG   _____

GRNAE   _____

EALID   _____

_____

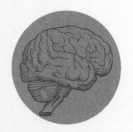

Teach a Class

Teach a continuing education class. In addition to the joy that comes with sharing your life wisdom, teaching helps strengthen mental function through reading, self-learning, and lecturing. Everyone is adept at something, so choose your specialty, approach a local continuing education program, and improve the world with your knowledge. You don't need a teaching degree, just experience.

Puzzle 14.09
Provider

3 LETTERS

ADD	PER
ASK	PHI
DAY	PIA
ELM	POP
ETA	POW
ICH	PRO
LIN	RID
ORC	RUE
OUR	RYE
OXO	TWO
OXY	URN
PEN	WOE

4 LETTERS

ACTA	ODDS
ACTS	ORCS
ALGA	PALE
ANAS	PIED
ANIL	PLUS
ARIL	PORK
BEER	PORN
CARE	RIDS
CODE	SCAM
COPE	SHAY
DEAR	SPUD
HIRE	TELS
IDLE	TOGA
INNS	TRAM
LEST	URGE
NOES	WIDE

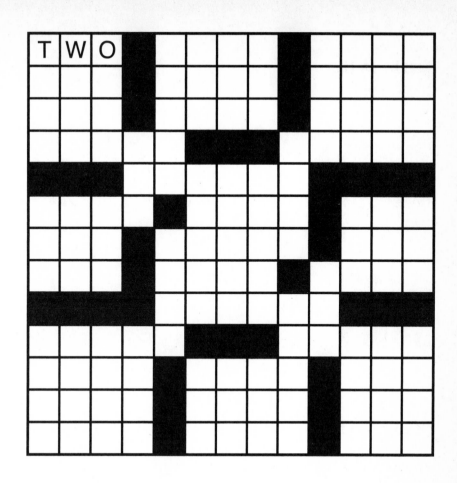

5 LETTERS

ASSET	MOLDS
ATRIA	ORCAS
EGEST	ORLES
LOSES	PASSE
MESAS	SCABS

6 LETTERS

CASTLE	SEAMEN

Puzzle 14.10

Cryptoquote

UAK ISBYH IK AZMK RBKZUKH DQ Z CBSHXRU ST

SXB UADPODPJ; DU RZPPSU GK RAZPJKH IDUASXU

RAZPJDPJ SXB UADPODPJ.

—ZYGKBU KDPQUKDP

Hint: The word "thinking" is found in the quote.

Puzzle 14.11

Cryptoquote

DMXVRPRB FU XV VMR JRAVRB SG SKB NFGR

DFNN QR VMR USKBJR SG SKB URJKBFVL,

WKFOXAJR, DFUOST, XAO HSDRB.

—UVRHMRA JSPRL

Hint: The word "wisdom" is found in the quote.

Puzzle 14.12

Crossword

Across

1. Mr. Claus
4. Spring or summer
7. Liquid rock
9. Back, at sea
10. Ugly duckling, ultimately
11. Read superficially
12. "Charlotte's ___"
14. Normandy campaign town
16. Above, in poetry
17. Red gem
19. ___ borealis (northern lights)
21. Many Mideasterners
22. Duo
23. ___ Canaveral
24. Get groceries
26. Ten years
29. ___ Lee (cake company)
31. Chauffeured vehicle
32. Acorn product
33. Lunch meat
34. Eskimo dwelling
35. Blossom
36. Opposite of max.
37. "___ Are My Sunshine"

Down

2. Tiny hill dwellers
3. Texas battle site of 1836
4. Emphatic assent in Acapulco
5. Detection device
6. Hammer's target
8. Woodchopper's tool
12. Christmas garland
13. Bridge calls
15. Gave a speech
18. Unbroken horse
19. Opera solos
20. "Gone With the Wind" surname
24. Not very often
25. Nonpoetic writing
27. Igloo dweller
28. Bride's walkway
30. Elbow's site
32. Yoko of music
33. Horse food

Puzzle 14.13
Sudoku

			2	4			5	3
	6			3	5			
4	3		7					9
						9		1
		8	5		9	3		
3		4						
1					2		9	7
			4	9			2	
5	2			7	8			

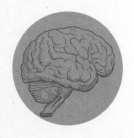

Eat More Wild Salmon

The omega-3 fatty acids present in salmon put this fish at the top of the superfoods chart. Salmon provides two types of omega-3s: DHA (docosahexaenoic acid) and EPA (eicosapentaenoic acid); and it's high in vitamin D, selenium, protein, and B vitamins. Some studies have found that omega-3s can significantly decrease serum triglyceride levels, lower blood pressure, and reduce blood levels of homocysteine, high levels of which are associated with an increased risk of Alzheimer's disease, among other conditions. The omega-3 fatty acids in salmon are essential for brain function, and eating a 4-ounce serving a couple of times a week will help improve your brain's agility.

Puzzle 14.14
Double Scramble

Light Lunch

SELTE   _____

EEGAR   _____

OISDC   _____

EOLMN   _____

EUSMA   _____

_____

Puzzle 14.15
Double Scramble

Casual Attire

ESHPE   _____

EJUIC   _____

WBELO   _____

ANNNY   _____

EFTAR   _____

_____

Puzzle 14.16
Sudoku

	7		8					
4	8	1	7		9			2
2			1		4		7	
8	9					6		
6								8
		3					2	4
	4		2		6			5
9			5		1	7	8	6
				7			4	

Puzzle 14.17
Sudoku

2	3		4	9		5	7	
							9	
					3		2	8
					4			1
	1	4	3	8	7	9	5	
3			1					
4	5		7					
	2							
	9	3		2	5		1	4

cow	lip
hammer	school
church	cart
box	muscle
match	bulb

Puzzle 14.18
Forget Me Not

_____   _____

_____   _____

_____   _____

_____   _____

_____   _____

What Was Your Time?

If you decided to challenge yourself further and time your puzzling session, be sure to write down your results below. Take a moment to reflect on your past sessions and acknowledge any improvements made along the way. With every chapter in this book, you should be able to notice how much more focused and alert your brain is becoming.

_____

_____

_____

_____

_____

_____

_____

_____

_____

_____

_____

_____

_____

_____

_____

_____

_____

_____

_____

CHAPTER 15

MEMORY LEVEL 15

bag	ball
pot	picture
hand	coat
knee	thread
bridge	boat

Puzzle 15.01
Forget Me Not

_____   _____

_____   _____

_____   _____

_____   _____

_____   _____

Puzzle 15.02
Provider

3 LETTERS

BRO	NIP
CHI	RUT
CUE	SEX
EAR	SKI
EGO	SOL
ELL	TWA
GHI	USE
GNU	UTA
HEW	WRY
IVY	YAR
LED	YOU
MOM	

4 LETTERS

AGHA	IDOL
ALEC	IRIS
ALTO	LENT
AUTO	LIMB
AVER	LOIN
AWRY	MILT
BALL	MYNA
BEAM	OGLE
BEGS	ORAL
BOIL	ORTS
CYST	PHEW
DOOR	RUSE
DRUM	SALS
DYNE	SCUM
HAKE	SLAY
HEAR	SUPS

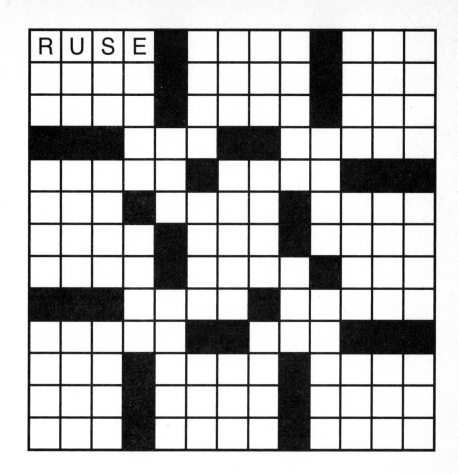

TEAR	TREE
TEXT	USES
TOYS	YAWP

5 LETTERS

ALPHA	RASPY
ESTER	SABRA
IONIC	SANTO
LAMBS	TATES
MADRE	

Puzzle 15.03
Cryptoquote

MPZMRO PDMWD OHGDXUCVI XH ZCOU AHT;

HXUDTZCOD RHF ZCPP KD GCODTMKPD ATHG RHFT

WDTR UMSSCVDOO.

—KMPXMOMT ITMJCMV

Hint: The word "otherwise" is found in the quote.

Minimize Alcohol Consumption

Most experts agree that a drink a day isn't health threatening, but abuse of alcohol or recreational drugs can diminish your ability to absorb stimuli from the world around you and result in a limited ability to form new memories. Brain scans of alcoholics tend to show low activity in the cerebellum, the brain's major coordination center. Alcohol should be consumed in moderation. Because it is considered a neurotoxin, heavy drinking can affect your health. Also, it's a harsh but true fact: Heavy use of alcohol has been associated with smaller brain volumes in people.

Puzzle 15.04
Crossword

Across

4. Bite like a pup
5. Go on all fours
6. Bambi and others
8. Brazilian ballroom dance
10. Actor George C.
11. Adam and Eve locale
13. Asner and Wynn
15. "Peter, Peter, Pumpkin ___"
18. Eiffel Tower city
20. Cave dwellers
22. Fictional work
24. Sly animal
25. ___ out a living (just gets by)
27. It's south of Ga.
28. Attaches, as a rope
29. Mil. entertainment group
31. Chocolate candy
33. Sound like a fan
34. X and Y on a graph
37. Blouse or shirt
39. Legal rights grp.
40. Cain's eldest son
41. River blocker
42. Good for what ___ you
43. Lawyers: abbr.

Down

1. Captain Kidd, for one
2. One of the five senses
3. North Pole toymaker
4. Home on a branch
5. Nickel or dime
6. Physicians, for short
7. Help a hoodlum
9. Very skilled
12. Clears the blackboard
14. Has the helm
16. Monastery heads
17. Sheets, tablecloths, etc.
19. Morse code message
21. X or Y, on a graph
23. Lobster's grabber
26. Where Seoul is
30. Rowing need
31. High-flying toys
32. De-wrinkle
35. "Get lost, kitty!"
36. Bombs that don't explode
38. "The Murders in the Rue Morgue" writer

Puzzle 15.05
Sudoku

9	3							
5		4	9		6			
		2			5			4
8	1			7			2	5
2	7			5			3	1
1			2			6		
			5		4	9		3
							5	2

Puzzle 15.06
Sudoku

4			7				2	
5	1							
9		2		8				3
2			8			9		
	4		1		6		5	
		5			4			6
7				1		3		2
							6	7
	3				2			1

Puzzle 15.07
Word Search

ANCHOVY
ANGEL
BARRACUDA
BASS
BLUEGILL
CARP
CATFISH
CHUB
CLAM
COD
CRAB
CRAPPIE
DOLPHIN
FLOUNDER
FLUKE
GOBY
GOLDFISH
GUPPY
HADDOCK
HALIBUT
JELLYFISH
LOBSTER
MACKEREL
MARLIN
MINNOW
MUSSEL
PERCH
PIKE
PUFFER
SALMON
SARDINE
SCALLOP

SEAL
SHARK
SNAPPER
SOLE
SPONGE
STARFISH
STURGEON
TROUT
TUNA
TURTLE
WALLEYE
WHALE
YELLOWTAIL

```
S T A R F I S H R S H A R K B R T A B P
G U P P Y O Y U S U S N A P P E R S E D
X B K G J A B Y D I I B H R L I A P L H
Y I M T U O O S E N F J H A Z L T P T L
T L B L U E G I L L Y D H C M L U R R E
M A R L I N C P T Q L W L O G E O B U S
Y H P E R C H O O U L O N O E G R U T S
H L A G T Z U D C E R W M G N T W E U
B H D N C R B K R M J M E T R A O A O M
K G O O U C B A R R A C U D A N L G E Q
R X D P L T P O L L A C S L N I T U Y Z
J G W S F P A P S S B P K I L U L V A N
O Z R R I U H B C A Z C M E E L O S B Y
A Y H E G F F I S R O A P I R H A L A A
R C K T I F L S N D A M A L C E H L F C
S I B S Y E E U D I O B Z N C Z L O I R
P D U B J R X A K N M C A T F I S H W N
D S T O U K H E Y E L L A W Z V N C V N
T C B L H J H I N R C M N Q B H U O S W
K N F Y S Z X S C L N Z S V K F S G D U
```

Puzzle 15.08
Double Scramble

Fuzzy Fruit

ONPTI _____

ACHKL _____

PAYPH _____

PETMY _____

LATAS _____

_____

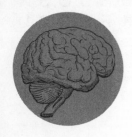

Eat More Avocados

Avocados contain monounsaturated fat known as oleic acid, which has been shown to help lower cholesterol, prevent heart disease and arteriosclerosis, and lower your risk for cancer. Avocados are also magnesium rich, as well as loaded with potassium, which helps regulate blood pressure and prevent circulatory diseases, including high blood pressure, stroke, and heart disease. One cup of avocado contains 23 percent of the daily value for folate, which, when combined with the monounsaturated fats plus potassium, decreases your chances of cardiovascular disease and stroke. Ounce for ounce, avocados provide more magnesium than do the twenty most commonly eaten fruits. They contain no starch and very little sugar, yet they provide an excellent source of usable food energy. However, one whole California avocado has over 300 calories and 35 grams of fat, 8.5 grams being monounsaturated fat, so eat small amounts for the optimum benefit.

Puzzle 15.09
Provider

3 LETTERS

ABS	NEE
ANY	NUB
BYE	OHS
CAN	OPE
DEE	PRY
DIP	REB
DUG	RUG
DUI	SUE
DYE	TUG
ERG	URB
GOA	YAY
HOW	ZOO
LIB	

4 LETTERS

ABBE	LIDO
ADOS	OGRE
ADZE	OWES
ALLY	PLAN
ASKS	POPS
BADE	POUT
BIOS	PURR
BOSS	SAGS
DEED	SECS
EELS	SEED
EGGS	SINE
EGGY	SLUE
EWER	SOAR
GUNK	SOUR
LEAP	SPOT

STEP	TROT
SUNS	TRUE
TARO	ULNA
TONG	WEBS

5 LETTERS

ADAGE	SPACE
APERS	SPEED
CREST	STATE
SLUES	

Puzzle 15.10
Cryptoquote

CV URNT FJ JFCZTB. FM FJ N ORCZTBMB

EYSBHJMNYSFYU RG MAB EYFKBHJB, XAV FM FJ

NJ FM FJ NYS XAV FM BWFJMJ NM NTT.

—JMBZABY ANXIFYU

Hint: The word "universe" is found in the quote.

Puzzle 15.11
Cryptoquote

KFJSJ BSJ PQOT KLP KSBMJEUJV UQ OUIJ: PQJ

UV QPK MJKKUQM LFBK PQJ LBQKV, BQE KFJ

PKFJS UV MJKKUQM UK.

—PVGBS LUOEJ

Hint: The word "tragedies" is found in the quote.

Puzzle 15.12
Crossword

Across

1. Prayer's end
2. Home audio system
7. In the ___ of luxury
9. Happy ___ lark
11. Collar, as a crook
13. Keep an ___ to the ground
15. Headache helper
18. Wild times
19. Judge's gown
20. Tennis champ Arthur
22. Scone spread
23. It replaced the lira
24. Eve's man
27. 1950s candidate Kefauver
29. Family friendly, in cinema
32. Winding road shape
34. Abbr.   before an alias
36. College website letters
38. Lawful, for short
39. School support org.
41. Road divisions
42. Ascots
44. Bricks measure
45. Boundary
47. Party attendees

Down

1. Palestinian leader
3. Oompah instrument
4. Sleep phenomenon: abbr.

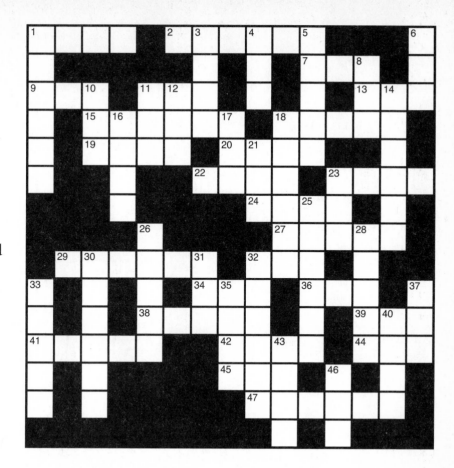

5. Song from the past
6. Not near
8. Household animal
10. Atmosphere
11. Omaha's state: abbr.
12. Lincoln or Vigoda
14. Houston baseballers
16. Baseball great Ty
17. Sal of song, e.g.
18. ___ Scholar
21. The Caribbean, e.g.
23. Ambulance driver, for short
25. Desirable qualities

26. Gets well
28. Blow, volcano-style
30. Lacking a key, in music
31. Comedian's bit
32. Restaurant activity
33. Not true
35. Paper-and-string flier
37. Mover's vehicle
40. Light throw
43. Part of HEW: abbr.
46. Dream Team jersey letters

Puzzle 15.13
Sudoku

			3		4			5
				2				3
1				6				8
	2			5			3	
		6	2		3	8		
	4			8			1	
8				3				4
6				1				
9			8		5			

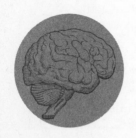

Express Gratitude

Focus on what you love about your life and your emotional brain fires up. You are more coordinated. Write out five things you're grateful for today. Focus on what is making you feel lucky and good about your life. This trains your brain to focus on the love and pleasant experiences in your life. Do it long enough, and you'll effectively create a positive groove in your brain that will produce ripple effects in your life.

Puzzle 15.14
Double Scramble

Not Napping

APELP   _____

OKNNW   _____

ELAIN   _____

THEGI   _____

ETRWA   _____

_____

Puzzle 15.15
Double Scramble

Elevator Stop

RXAEL   _____

AOSIS   _____

ISFTR   _____

ILGHT   _____

RFOEF   _____

_____

Puzzle 15.16
Sudoku

7	6		3					8
							5	
	8			1	7	3	9	
3			6		2			5
	9			8			7	
4			9		3			2
	4	1	8	2			3	
	7							
8					4		6	1

Puzzle 15.17
Sudoku

	2						9	
	6	1	3				2	4
5		7	4					3
		4						7
7	3			1			5	2
1					8			
2					1	3		9
3	1				7	2	4	
	7					6		

whistle	eye
brain	arm
shirt	carriage
sponge	star
rat	feather

Puzzle 15.18
Forget Me Not

_____   _____

_____   _____

_____   _____

_____   _____

_____   _____

What Was Your Time?

If you decided to challenge yourself further and time your puzzling session, be sure to write down your results below. Take a moment to reflect on your past sessions and acknowledge any improvements made along the way. With every chapter in this book, you should be able to notice how much more focused and alert your brain is becoming.

_____

_____

_____

_____

_____

_____

_____

_____

_____

_____

_____

_____

_____

_____

_____

_____

ANSWERS

ANSWER 1.02

R	E	P		B	A	R	B		G	O	L	D
O	A	R		A	L	E	E		A	R	I	A
C	U	E		L	A	S	E		T	A	R	P
		S	A	L	S	A		C	E	D	E	S
R	I	A	L	S		L	O	O	S			
U	R	G	E		P	E	R	T		P	A	S
S	I	E	S	T	A		L	E	A	R	N	T
E	S	S		E	R	N	E		N	O	T	A
		T	A	T	E		C	A	T	E	R	
A	C	M	E	S		A	R	O	S	E		
L	O	A	N		E	R	O	S		S	H	H
T	O	Y	S		R	E	S	T		T	A	O
S	L	O	E		A	R	E	S		S	E	E

ANSWER 1.03

In the end, we will remember not the words of our enemies, but the silence of our friends.

—Martin Luther King Jr.

ANSWER 1.04

ANSWER 1.05

8	9	2	7	1	5	6	3	4
4	1	5	3	9	6	7	2	8
3	7	6	4	2	8	9	5	1
7	6	8	2	5	9	1	4	3
9	4	1	8	3	7	2	6	5
2	5	3	6	4	1	8	9	7
6	8	9	5	7	3	4	1	2
1	3	4	9	8	2	5	7	6
5	2	7	1	6	4	3	8	9

ANSWER 1.06

3	4	9	8	2	6	5	7	1
1	5	8	4	7	3	9	2	6
7	6	2	5	9	1	8	4	3
9	8	4	1	5	2	6	3	7
2	3	1	7	6	8	4	9	5
5	7	6	9	3	4	2	1	8
8	2	3	6	4	7	1	5	9
6	9	7	2	1	5	3	8	4
4	1	5	3	8	9	7	6	2

ANSWER 1.07

ANSWER 1.08

CIVIL	HOTEL	ANNOY
TOWEL	MERCY	MATCH

ANSWER 1.09

S	O	S		S	E	C	S		A	P	O	D
A	R	E		L	O	O	P		S	A	R	I
T	E	E		A	N	N	A		S	L	A	G
	S	P	A	T		S	A	E				
		P	S	S	T		S	T	A	B	S	
L	O	S	E		O	A	K	S		S	E	A
A	N	E	S		R	I	A		C	E	E	S
N	E	T		S	E	L	L		O	A	T	S
E	S	T	E	R		S	E	E	D			
		N	I	P			S	A	P	S		
S	H	A	D		A	D	O	S		H	O	T
P	A	G	E		L	U	X	E		A	L	A
A	P	E	D		S	O	Y	S		T	O	R

ANSWER 1.10

Love vanquishes time. To lovers, a moment can be eternity, eternity can be the tick of a clock.

—Mary Parrish

ANSWER 1.11

Everyone is a genius at least once a year. A real genius has his original ideas closer together.

—Georg C. Lichtenberg

ANSWER 1.12

```
S U M O   O N E                 O
  T   R A W           E   R A T
R E B U S     L   C A L L A     I
  A     O         F L A N       S
  K I D N A P     L I A M     S
    E     L   S     R     O   N
  H E N R I       A V E R T     O
  I   S     A I R         T A B
  K N E E   S T A M I N A
    T     A   S       O   N A P
      A N N O Y       T H A I
S E W   Y     H     R E T R O
  B E N       A   T E A     E
  A       S A L S A   R O S S
S Y R U P             C
```

ANSWER 1.13

9	2	3	4	5	6	8	7	1
8	5	1	9	3	7	4	6	2
7	6	4	2	1	8	9	3	5
1	7	2	8	9	5	3	4	6
6	3	8	1	4	2	7	5	9
4	9	5	7	6	3	1	2	8
5	8	9	3	2	4	6	1	7
2	4	7	6	8	1	5	9	3
3	1	6	5	7	9	2	8	4

ANSWER 1.14

HEARD	RADIO	ADULT
COLOR	NEVER	RANCH

ANSWER 1.15

ENJOY	LOYAL	REACH
ANKLE	GLIDE	LARGE

ANSWER 1.16

8	4	7	1	6	2	5	9	3
5	6	1	3	7	9	2	4	8
9	3	2	4	8	5	7	1	6
6	7	3	8	2	4	9	5	1
1	5	9	7	3	6	4	8	2
2	8	4	5	9	1	6	3	7
7	1	6	9	5	3	8	2	4
4	2	5	6	1	8	3	7	9
3	9	8	2	4	7	1	6	5

ANSWER 1.17

3	7	4	9	5	6	2	8	1
2	9	5	1	3	8	6	7	4
1	6	8	4	7	2	5	9	3
8	1	2	7	9	4	3	5	6
6	4	3	8	1	5	9	2	7
9	5	7	2	6	3	4	1	8
4	8	9	3	2	7	1	6	5
5	3	1	6	8	9	7	4	2
7	2	6	5	4	1	8	3	9

ANSWER 2.02

```
S C A T     A R M     A S P S
L O N E     L O O     S H E A
A R T S     P O D     S E A L
T E A T         T E L E
        A S P         E S T O P
A R C     P O R T S     O L E
L I E     A L I A S     D I N
L O P     R O B L E     S O T
S T E T S       L E T
      E E L S         S A D E
A M P S     A H A     A R E A
R O U T     M I X     R I M S
T A G S     A N E     S L O T
```

ANSWER 2.03

Immature love says: I love you because I need you. Mature love says: I need you because I love you.

—Erich Fromm

ANSWER 2.04

```
                    I A N
                  Y E S   O R E
                    B O I S E
              E R R O L   E V A
        B       M   A L A
  H E E       B E R A T E   C
A B B A   R E N E     E L B O W
R O B     I R S         I R A
K     O   N     N         A S S
A   P A S T A     R   U N T O
N   S M E A R     O         N
S I T   E   C E D A R   G
A     A L S O   A D O   A P E
S U M M I T     N I N E S   E
  P A Y     T A E           L
```

ANSWER 2.05

6	1	9	8	7	5	2	4	3
2	7	4	6	3	9	5	8	1
3	8	5	4	2	1	9	6	7
1	5	3	9	4	2	6	7	8
8	2	6	7	1	3	4	5	9
4	9	7	5	8	6	3	1	2
5	3	2	1	6	7	8	9	4
7	6	8	2	9	4	1	3	5
9	4	1	3	5	8	7	2	6

ANSWER 2.06

```
8 3 7 9 6 2 4 1 5
9 5 6 7 1 4 8 3 2
2 1 4 8 5 3 7 6 9
5 8 3 4 7 9 6 2 1
1 7 2 5 8 6 9 4 3
4 6 9 3 2 1 5 8 7
7 9 1 2 4 8 3 5 6
6 4 5 1 3 7 2 9 8
3 2 8 6 9 5 1 7 4
```

ANSWER 2.07

```
L M A G I C J O H N S O N M L N A Y D R
J O H N N Y U N I T A S C A O H B K A E
S M A I L L I W D E T F R T N M A R R V
X S D N O B Y R R A B R Y O X R K E N S A
I N G N N H Q T D G Y A S R E H E N S L
F N N A I N L W C I R I T M K R E M A D O
U A I M H R W C I R I T M K R E M A A O
Z M W N I A L R E B M A H C T L I W S R
Z S E O H M O T O E B R K E H L C S R S
Y I K T J O L R S D I K R B U I H U E U
Z E C Y S A E O U S A E U S R M A N D A
O H I E W I R L S N V N Q I A E E O N L
E T R P K E J A A A J T V R S I L H A K
L E C T A G G E Y R O J O H G J N S C C
L O A E B A O S C M V N N B E G O U N I
E J P B E H M O A L L E N I V E R S O N
R Y A R N O L D P A L M E R D R D U I K
P D E T T E R R Y B R A D S H A W E C
N N B R G Y J U L I U S E R V I N G D A
A S A M O H T A I S I B I X O E D K J
```

ANSWER 2.08

BASIC	KARMA	CARGO
RAISE	INDIA	**BRICK**

ANSWER 2.09

```
H U T . . T R O T . O H S
E T A S . A E R O . L E A
M A N O . S E E R . D A M
. . L A S S . T A S T E
M A T E R . . P S I .
A G O . B A B A . L A B S
S U M . S C A R S . P I U
T E E D . M A S H . E K E
. . O S E . M A R E S
T A C E T . S T O W .
A L E . A L O E . L A P S
P A N . R I C E . S T O A
S E T . T S K S . T I C
```

ANSWER 2.10

Wise men talk because they have something to say; fools, because they have to say something.

—Plato

ANSWER 2.11

Analyzing humor is like dissecting a frog. Few people are interested and the frog dies of it.

—E. B. White

ANSWER 2.12

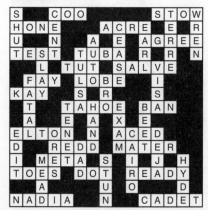

ANSWER 2.13

```
1 5 9 3 7 6 2 8 4
7 3 4 8 9 2 6 1 5
6 2 8 4 5 1 3 7 9
8 1 5 7 6 9 4 2 3
9 7 3 5 2 4 8 6 1
2 4 6 1 3 8 9 5 7
4 9 1 6 8 7 5 3 2
3 8 7 2 4 5 1 9 6
5 6 2 9 1 3 7 4 8
```

ANSWER 2.14

HOBBY	URBAN	MAPLE
ALARM	NIGHT	**HUMAN**

ANSWER 2.15

CHAIN	AGENT	NORTH
INDEX	BEACH	**CABIN**

ANSWER 2.16

```
1 4 3 2 9 7 5 6 8
5 2 7 4 8 6 9 3 1
6 9 8 1 5 3 4 7 2
7 5 9 3 2 1 8 4 6
4 3 1 5 6 8 2 9 7
8 6 2 9 7 4 3 1 5
9 1 5 6 4 2 7 8 3
3 7 4 8 1 5 6 2 9
2 8 6 7 3 9 1 5 4
```

ANSWER 2.17

6	2	8	7	9	1	3	5	4
1	3	4	8	6	5	7	2	9
7	9	5	4	3	2	8	6	1
5	1	7	9	4	8	6	3	2
9	4	3	5	2	6	1	8	7
2	8	6	3	1	7	9	4	5
8	7	1	2	5	3	4	9	6
3	5	9	6	7	4	2	1	8
4	6	2	1	8	9	5	7	3

ANSWER 3.02

T	H	E		L	O	W	E		S	I	R	E
A	I	R		A	W	A	Y		H	O	A	R
E	N	G		S	E	R	E		A	N	T	S
	T	O	P	E		S	O	L				
		A	R	C	S		S	T	A	F	F	
S	T	A	T		H	A	T	E		B	O	O
H	O	N		G	I	R	O	S		B	E	N
O	N	S		L	A	I	R		B	E	S	T
P	E	A	S	E		S	O	R	A			
		E	E	L		E	T	H	S			
M	E	A	T		A	M	A	S		A	L	B
A	L	I	T		D	O	G	E		S	U	E
E	L	M	S		S	W	A	T		T	E	L

ANSWER 3.03

Outside of a dog, a book is a man's best friend. Inside of a dog, it is too dark to read.

—Groucho Marx

ANSWER 3.04

ANSWER 3.05

1	5	8	4	6	3	7	2	9
3	4	7	9	2	5	8	1	6
2	9	6	1	7	8	4	5	3
5	6	2	7	9	4	1	3	8
4	8	3	5	1	6	9	7	2
7	1	9	3	8	2	5	6	4
6	7	1	8	3	9	2	4	5
9	2	4	6	5	1	3	8	7
8	3	5	2	4	7	6	9	1

ANSWER 3.06

6	3	5	9	2	4	1	7	8
8	7	4	6	1	5	3	2	9
1	9	2	3	8	7	6	5	4
5	4	1	8	6	3	2	9	7
9	2	7	5	4	1	8	6	3
3	8	6	7	9	2	5	4	1
7	1	3	4	5	6	9	8	2
4	6	9	2	3	8	7	1	5
2	5	8	1	7	9	4	3	6

ANSWER 3.07

ANSWER 3.08

ALERT   EXACT   PARTY

PANIC   RAPID   **PAPER**

ANSWER 3.09

A	I	L	S		A	W	L		C	H	I	N
B	R	I	T		P	I	A		L	A	M	E
S	E	T	A		S	T	Y		A	L	A	N
		R	U	E				S	O	M	E	
A	P	S	E	S		E	R	R	S			
T	I	E		A	L	L	E	E		T	W	A
O	C	A		B	E	A	S	T		S	I	R
M	A	R		L	A	T	H	E		A	R	K
			M	E	R	E		A	C	R	E	S
A	C	H	E				B	R	R			
L	O	O	T		E	R	E		A	T	O	P
T	I	N	E		T	O	T		S	O	D	A
O	L	E	S		H	E	S		S	E	E	M

ANSWER 3.10

Love doesn't just sit there like a stone; it has to be made, like bread, remade all the time, made new.

—Ursula K. LeGuin

ANSWER 3.11

What we call the secret of happiness is no more a secret than our willingness to choose life.

—Leo Buscaglia

ANSWER 3.12

```
A . . . P I T Y . . U . . . F
T O F U . A . A . . N . P R O
M . . S U R R . Y O D A . E .
. . D E T E S T . . . I N C .
B E E . A . A . O L G A . . .
A . L . H U G E . K . I C E .
I . . S E P A R A T E . . . A
L O C A T E . . I V A N . . .
. . . D . D E C O . W . . . S
N . B A D . . . I R A N . . L
B O O P . L . A D O R E . . I
A . S T R E E P . . A . M A T
S . . F . P . D O O R . . . P
. . . T A L E S . . . I . O .
O R N E R Y . . E . . E N D E D
```

ANSWER 3.13

6	7	9	5	4	1	8	2	3
1	5	2	8	3	9	6	7	4
4	8	3	2	6	7	9	5	1
5	3	4	1	9	2	7	8	6
9	1	8	6	7	3	5	4	2
7	2	6	4	5	8	1	3	9
3	6	7	9	8	4	2	1	5
2	4	5	7	1	6	3	9	8
8	9	1	3	2	5	4	6	7

ANSWER 3.14

ORGAN   STONE   LEARN
STAMP   ADMIT   **LASSO**

ANSWER 3.15

GAUGE   SNAKE   ACTOR
RAINY   SPOON   **GRASS**

ANSWER 3.16

3	4	2	8	6	9	7	1	5
8	1	7	5	3	2	9	6	4
5	6	9	1	4	7	8	3	2
9	2	1	4	8	6	3	5	7
6	8	5	7	1	3	4	2	9
4	7	3	2	9	5	6	8	1
7	5	4	6	2	8	1	9	3
2	9	6	3	7	1	5	4	8
1	3	8	9	5	4	2	7	6

ANSWER 3.17

2	7	6	5	9	8	3	4	1
8	4	1	2	7	3	6	9	5
5	9	3	4	1	6	8	7	2
7	3	8	6	2	4	5	1	9
6	1	4	9	8	5	7	2	3
9	5	2	7	3	1	4	8	6
1	6	5	8	4	9	2	3	7
3	8	7	1	5	2	9	6	4
4	2	9	3	6	7	1	5	8

ANSWER 4.02

```
A L B S . S O W S . . T W O
T A U T . A G E E . . H O W
E T N A . B E E N . . A V E
. . . T H E E . S A T E S .
S C R E E . . T E D . . . .
C O O . L O D E . S A N E .
A M P . L U R E S . R E G .
D E E D . T Y N E . M A G .
. . O R S . . C A S T S .
P A S T E . M A T E . . .
O U T . S H A Y . D A D O
P R O . T A L E . E L A N
S A P . S H E S . S T Y E
```

ANSWER 4.03

A great many people think they are thinking when they are merely rearranging their prejudices.

—William James

ANSWER 4.04

```
R E E S E . T I S . V . P .
A . P . . . . P L A Z A . M
P . R E N T . O . I . L I E
O E . O R I O N . L . . . M
W I E N E R . L . . E C H O
E . A . N . . . . . H . . .
. P A P U A . F . U N I T E
E R R A N D . L A P . N . R
A L E C . C O L U M B I A . I
. A . L . E . B E T . . . C
P . N E E . O . E A S E L .
A S H E . B . A R T . V E E
W E E . A L E . N . . V I A
A . A . S . S . N . . L S D
Y . L . H U S S E I N . . T
```

ANSWER 4.05

6	5	4	9	1	7	8	3	2
1	3	2	8	6	4	5	9	7
7	8	9	2	3	5	1	4	6
9	2	7	3	5	1	4	6	8
5	4	1	6	9	8	7	2	3
8	6	3	4	7	2	9	1	5
2	7	5	1	4	6	3	8	9
3	1	8	5	2	9	6	7	4
4	9	6	7	8	3	2	5	1

ANSWER 4.06

5	3	1	2	9	6	4	8	7
9	2	4	3	8	7	6	5	1
7	8	6	4	1	5	3	9	2
4	7	5	9	3	1	8	2	6
3	9	2	7	6	8	5	1	4
6	1	8	5	2	4	7	3	9
2	5	9	6	4	3	1	7	8
8	6	7	1	5	2	9	4	3
1	4	3	8	7	9	2	6	5

ANSWER 4.07

```
C K M U B Y Z P A P A Y A R K O B C E H
M P E B O R R A A Y E N M P H K H D V I
Q G L E Z F G R E E N P E P P E R A W Z
L N O M M I S R E P U O L A T N A C T Q
F Z N I N N E N V B L B P C O C O N U T
L N Z U I X I K R R N S I L O C C O R B
K G W P P R K E O L R E L P P A J L N L
O U Y A E E P A H G E S V S D G E I O
X A M G T M A M H C I B Y S N R M P M
A V N K U E F C A U L I F L O W E R M P
B A X R P H C P Q T U B E E W Z
T B U R T L X J K K O U R Y M N T C B
A C P U R X I C R L B B T H A R B A X A
U W C J C E T E E B N E A C N E W U D
Q E R O N U B S N B S D O R T A A L X J
M Y T F L O O N B E G S I I R O N N E M
U X A I M U L P A R L E M O N Y S I A C
K M T A A N E Y R R E B N A G O L Y P B
K R A S P B E R R Y C A R R O T U G Z S
F U G V H Y X T I F V X L Y M D Z P P N
```

ANSWER 4.08

REPLY	TEASE	IDIOT
KAYAK	CATCH	**TRICK**

ANSWER 4.09

B	R	O		B	E	N	T		B	A	L	E
R	I	D		A	L	A	R		L	I	E	N
A	P	E		S	K	E	E		A	D	D	S
G	E	S	T	E			E	L	S			
		O	R	T	S		A	T	L	A	S	
C	A	S	E		I	L	K	S		A	N	A
A	W	E	S		L	E	I		L	I	O	N
T	O	M		S	E	E	N		I	N	N	S
S	L	I	C	E		T	E	S	T			
		A	N	T				T	E	M	P	S
O	W	N	S		E	P	E	E		Y	E	A
H	O	O	T		N	A	V	E		T	R	Y
M	O	T	E		S	P	E	D		H	I	S

ANSWER 4.10

He who controls the present, controls the past. He who controls the past, controls the future.

—George Orwell

ANSWER 4.11

People grow through experience if they meet life honestly and courageously. This is how character is built.

—Eleanor Roosevelt

ANSWER 4.12

	D	E	E	R			A			A	L	U	M
		D	E	N	I	M		B	E	T	A		Y
S	A	L	E	M		A		Y		E	D	G	E
A		U	N	I		A	R	I	E	L		L	R
N		R		T	E	R	I			F	E	S	S
D	I	E			E	L	E	C	T				
	G			S	A	L	T		S				
	L	A	D	E	N		O	C	C	U	R		K
L	O	O			I			N	I	K	E		
Y	O	R	E		P	E	S	O		A	T	O	N	E
S		T	N	T		O			O	M	A	R		Z
O	V	A	L			S	E	M	I		E		R
L			I	P	O		E			J	A	V	A
	P	B	S		V		N		I				
		T	E	A	S	E		S		B	A	H	

ANSWER 4.13

1	9	4	7	8	5	2	6	3
3	8	7	4	2	6	5	9	1
6	2	5	9	1	3	4	7	8
8	3	6	1	5	4	7	2	9
9	4	1	2	6	7	8	3	5
5	7	2	8	3	9	1	4	6
2	6	3	5	7	1	9	8	4
4	1	8	3	9	2	6	5	7
7	5	9	6	4	8	3	1	2

ANSWER 4.14

NOISY	TASTY	INPUT
ALOUD	GRADE	**GIANT**

ANSWER 4.15

VIDEO	GLOVE	ARGUE
ENEMY	UPSET	**VAGUE**

ANSWER 4.16

9	5	6	8	2	1	4	7	3
4	3	8	5	7	6	1	9	2
1	7	2	9	3	4	5	8	6
2	8	3	1	6	9	7	5	4
6	1	7	2	4	5	8	3	9
5	4	9	7	8	3	6	2	1
7	6	4	3	9	8	2	1	5
8	9	5	6	1	2	3	4	7
3	2	1	4	5	7	9	6	8

ANSWER 4.17

1	5	2	9	4	7	3	6	8
3	4	6	2	8	1	9	7	5
8	9	7	5	3	6	2	1	4
4	2	8	1	7	5	6	9	3
9	3	1	4	6	8	5	2	7
6	7	5	3	9	2	4	8	1
5	1	4	7	2	9	8	3	6
7	6	9	8	5	3	1	4	2
2	8	3	6	1	4	7	5	9

ANSWER 5.02

ANSWER 5.03

Life is to be lived, not controlled, and humanity is won by continuing to play in face of certain defeat.

—Ralph Ellison

ANSWER 5.04

ANSWER 5.05

4	1	2	6	8	5	3	7	9
6	3	7	9	4	1	2	8	5
9	8	5	7	2	3	4	6	1
8	2	9	4	1	7	5	3	6
7	6	4	3	5	2	1	9	8
3	5	1	8	6	9	7	2	4
5	9	6	2	7	4	8	1	3
1	7	8	5	3	6	9	4	2
2	4	3	1	9	8	6	5	7

ANSWER 5.06

7	1	3	9	5	4	6	8	2
6	8	4	2	1	7	5	9	3
9	5	2	8	6	3	1	7	4
3	9	1	5	4	8	2	6	7
8	4	7	6	2	1	3	5	9
2	6	5	3	7	9	4	1	8
5	2	9	7	3	6	8	4	1
1	7	6	4	8	2	9	3	5
4	3	8	1	9	5	7	2	6

ANSWER 5.07

ANSWER 5.08

OPERA   MAYBE   OLIVE

RIVER   TASTE   MOTOR

ANSWER 5.09

ANSWER 5.10

We are made wise not by the recollection of our past, but by the responsibility for our future.

—George Bernard Shaw

ANSWER 5.11

Half our life is spent trying to find something to do with the time we have rushed through life trying to save.

—Will Rogers

ANSWER 5.12

ANSWER 5.13

1	8	4	9	5	2	6	3	7
5	7	3	1	6	4	8	9	2
6	2	9	8	3	7	5	1	4
2	4	8	7	1	5	3	6	9
3	6	5	4	8	9	2	7	1
7	9	1	3	2	6	4	5	8
8	5	2	6	7	1	9	4	3
9	3	7	5	4	8	1	2	6
4	1	6	2	9	3	7	8	5

ANSWER 5.14

WHEEL	SHORT	TEACH
TENTH	IGLOO	TWIST

ANSWER 5.15

THUMB	IMAGE	EBONY
LOVED	RHYME	LITER

ANSWER 5.16

7	6	8	5	4	2	1	3	9
1	9	4	8	3	7	5	2	6
3	2	5	6	1	9	4	8	7
6	4	9	1	5	8	3	7	2
2	3	1	9	7	4	8	6	5
5	8	7	3	2	6	9	1	4
4	1	2	7	8	5	6	9	3
9	5	3	2	6	1	7	4	8
8	7	6	4	9	3	2	5	1

ANSWER 5.17

7	1	9	6	3	5	8	4	2
8	6	5	2	1	4	9	3	7
3	4	2	7	9	8	1	5	6
1	8	7	9	4	3	6	2	5
5	9	4	1	2	6	3	7	8
2	3	6	5	8	7	4	1	9
4	2	8	3	5	9	7	6	1
9	7	1	4	6	2	5	8	3
6	5	3	8	7	1	2	9	4

ANSWER 6.02

```
O F F S _ C H I S _ B E T
P E A T _ A U N T _ R A W
S Y N E _ P E K E _ A V A
_ _ A L S _ _ N O T E S
S A B L E _ P R O A _
P R Y _ G L U E _ R A F T
I C E S _ A M A _ S A L E
N O S E _ T A R T _ H E T
_ _ A C E S _ E A S E S
B A S S O _ _ M A N _
I C E _ L O G E _ G N A T
E R R _ T O O T _ S O N E
R E F _ S H O E _ T W I N
```

ANSWER 6.03

The happiest moments of my life have been the few which I have passed at home in the bosom of my family.

—Thomas Jefferson

ANSWER 6.04

ANSWER 6.05

5	7	3	9	1	2	8	6	4
2	4	1	8	6	7	9	5	3
6	9	8	4	5	3	7	2	1
7	5	6	1	8	4	3	9	2
4	3	9	2	7	5	6	1	8
1	8	2	3	9	6	5	4	7
8	2	5	6	3	1	4	7	9
9	1	7	5	4	8	2	3	6
3	6	4	7	2	9	1	8	5

ANSWER 6.06

1	8	9	5	3	2	7	4	6
4	7	5	9	6	8	2	3	1
2	3	6	4	1	7	9	5	8
6	5	2	1	8	9	4	7	3
8	4	1	3	7	5	6	9	2
3	9	7	6	2	4	8	1	5
9	6	4	2	5	3	1	8	7
7	1	3	8	4	6	5	2	9
5	2	8	7	9	1	3	6	4

ANSWER 6.07

```
D J L E W O P D T Z S J X P H W K R W B
E I G O P H L Q Q H W W R M P X N W L G
E B V O K O S Z X N I A R D I C A S W F
L W C E C Y H Y Y D U O L C T G G I O A
X L I W Q Q R U P T T X T S O R F G B K
I W A N S E W O N S G N I W O L B J N L
U N Y F D F K C T B S G N I N T H G I L
E O N N N Y X S S N O W F A L L J J A S
J Q U O I X U J R L T M C Q N C M T R Z
H H Z U W D A A Q E R R B O I W E O T Q
P X K T V E R E O B P M Q A J N R U N
A Y I A E L O L W E A T H E R V A N E O
R T A I C E S T O R M J V R G N C A N D
T W E A T H E R B A L L O O N L I D O R
T P R E C I P I T A T I O N I K R O L Z
T F M G B J D V T Q U E Z M Z W R B C I Z
B X J A L L T Q H S S K A S E L U Z Y Z
V A D D O O N D W K X X Y D E I H P C L
G F R Y J P R J M T E M P E R A T U R E
H W F U T B A V V S D O O L F H X U Z B
```

ANSWER 6.08

GUEST	RIGHT	ULCER
APPLY	SEVEN	SUGAR

ANSWER 6.09

```
M I N D   . E M S .   B E R G
A L O W . R A N .   A G H A
T I R E . G N U .   R O O M
T A M E .   A G A R .
.   B U R G .   R I F T S
C A W . N E E .   M E L E E
I R I S E S . P A R A D E
T I N E A . D I D .   T S K
E D G E S . R E A M .
.   R E P O .   A C T S
A B L E . U G H .   S O I L
F O Y S . R U M . T O R A
T Y E S . R E M .   S N O W
```

ANSWER 6.10

The mind is its own place, and in itself, can make heaven of Hell, and a hell of Heaven.

—John Milton

ANSWER 6.11

Nearly all men can stand adversity, but if you want to test a man's character, give him power.

—Abraham Lincoln

ANSWER 6.12

ANSWER 6.13

2	6	7	5	8	1	4	9	3
1	3	8	9	6	4	7	5	2
9	4	5	7	3	2	1	6	8
4	5	3	6	7	9	2	8	1
6	7	2	1	4	8	5	3	9
8	9	1	3	2	5	6	4	7
7	1	4	8	9	6	3	2	5
5	2	9	4	1	3	8	7	6
3	8	6	2	5	7	9	1	4

ANSWER 6.14

LEVEL	UNION	NOISE
ABOVE	READY	LUNAR

ANSWER 6.15

DAISY	ARRAY	RAVEN
ELDER	BENCH	BREAD

ANSWER 6.16

9	8	3	2	4	6	1	5	7
1	5	6	3	9	7	4	2	8
2	4	7	1	5	8	6	3	9
6	9	5	4	2	1	7	8	3
7	3	1	6	8	9	5	4	2
4	2	8	7	3	5	9	6	1
5	1	4	8	7	2	3	9	6
3	6	2	9	1	4	8	7	5
8	7	9	5	6	3	2	1	4

ANSWER 6.17

3	4	2	8	6	7	9	5	1
7	9	6	3	1	5	2	4	8
8	5	1	9	4	2	3	7	6
9	3	5	1	7	8	6	2	4
2	7	4	6	9	3	1	8	5
6	1	8	2	5	4	7	3	9
4	6	3	5	2	1	8	9	7
5	8	9	7	3	6	4	1	2
1	2	7	4	8	9	5	6	3

ANSWER 7.02

E	F	T		S	P	A	N		C	A	R	D
D	I	E		L	E	N	O		U	V	E	A
G	A	R		A	N	D	S		B	E	N	D
E	T	N	A	S				P	E	S	T	S
			C	H	A	R	G	E				
B	A	B	E		G	I	R	T		S	P	Y
A	B	O		O	G	L	E	S		H	I	E
L	A	D		P	I	L	E		B	A	G	S
			T	E	E	N	S	Y				
W	A	S	P	S				T	E	M	P	T
H	E	A	R		B	A	K	E		O	U	R
Y	O	G	I		A	N	I	L		O	P	E
S	N	A	G		D	Y	N	E		R	A	Y

ANSWER 7.03

Do not follow where the path may lead.
Go instead where there is no path and
leave a trail.
— Ralph Waldo Emerson

ANSWER 7.04

A	B	Y	S	S		A		H			G			
C				C	O	B	R	A		S	I	A	M	
H	O	N	O	R		L		I	R	O	N			
E				A	X	E		K		D				
		R	O	M			L	U	C	A	S		E	
A		I				R		E		N			N	
V	I	N	E			A		N					E	
I						T	I	E	D				M	
S	A	M		S	M	O	G		S	O	Y			
	R			B	E	A	T		L		R			
T	E	D			E	R	O	D	E		E			
	N		D	E	N	S			S	L	O	T		
P	A	B	L	O				C	I	T	E		I	
	I		M	O	V	E			S	I	L	L		
C	R	O	P			A	M	E	S		E			

ANSWER 7.05

6	5	9	4	2	1	8	7	3
4	7	2	3	6	8	5	9	1
1	3	8	9	7	5	6	2	4
2	1	3	5	9	7	4	6	8
9	8	6	2	3	4	1	5	7
7	4	5	8	1	6	9	3	2
8	9	7	1	5	2	3	4	6
5	2	4	6	8	3	7	1	9
3	6	1	7	4	9	2	8	5

ANSWER 7.06

3	6	8	7	1	5	9	2	4
9	5	1	2	6	4	7	8	3
7	2	4	3	8	9	1	6	5
2	7	6	5	4	1	3	9	8
8	4	9	6	3	7	5	1	2
1	3	5	9	2	8	4	7	6
5	8	3	1	9	2	6	4	7
6	1	2	4	7	3	8	5	9
4	9	7	8	5	6	2	3	1

ANSWER 7.07

```
L H G J W E S U O M J T Q L Q V S M M M
N H P N Y X L O T D C E N I P U C R O P
X L E P E D I G R E E I A E M E P D N K
P L P V N F C A C E S O L A L O P B G Z
W U P K E O P T K K X I T O R I T F O X
P R A C C O O N U U B O O A O D T I O P
C H F U E R G N C R P E N P N L V P S S
S I Y L R D K I E O K M C I R D P A E V
E O C A T T C G P A C H O P H O Y H R R
Q P Q I N H P N A R K Z K W R P U I K
I E N G A A I S D E E A A G E C K O G N
A Y E X O U N Y B A T N B T L H T D T U
U R Y R J P C F A P S T I B I E W A L M
Q A Y A T E H B D R M W U I E A G I P
J A M T C L I L G X A E Z K G T L R H I
D C G A Z E L L E O H M L I Z A R D N H
T W M U L T L K R Y D A N E Y H U G E C
X E R N A L A E N C Z X B I D G S R B L
L A O I F R B O Z P U R N R U V J U X H
M D L H D B P M G A A X H Q G L B N Z J
```

ANSWER 7.08

ANGRY	COUGH	HONEY
ORBIT	NIFTY	NACHO

ANSWER 7.09

E	N	D		A	N	T	I		A	B	R	I
W	A	Y		R	E	I	N		B	R	A	D
E	Y	E	D	R	O	P	S		B	A	N	E
			R	A	N	T		H	E	E	D	S
M	I	C	A	S		O	P	E	S			
E	L	H	I		D	E	E	R		S	K	I
S	E	A	N	C	E		C	O	S	T	A	R
H	A	D		L	A	G	S		L	U	N	K
			S	O	L	I		C	O	D	E	S
S	E	W	E	D		G	R	O	G			
L	Y	R	E		W	O	O	D	S	M	A	N
I	R	E	D		A	L	M	A		E	Y	E
P	E	N	S		S	O	P	S		D	E	B

ANSWER 7.10

The important thing is not to stop
questioning. Curiosity has its own reason
for existing.
— Albert Einstein

ANSWER 7.11

A kiss is a lovely trick designed by nature to stop speech when words become superfluous.

—Ingrid Bergman

ANSWER 7.12

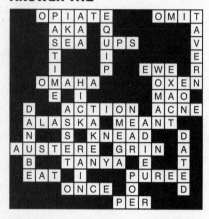

ANSWER 7.13

1	2	8	7	4	9	3	5	6
7	4	6	5	3	2	8	1	9
5	3	9	6	1	8	4	7	2
9	1	3	4	7	6	2	8	5
6	5	2	8	9	1	7	3	4
8	7	4	3	2	5	6	9	1
2	8	7	9	5	4	1	6	3
3	9	1	2	6	7	5	4	8
4	6	5	1	8	3	9	2	7

ANSWER 7.14

ORDER	ABORT	OCCUR
KHAKI	ZEBRA	KAZOO

ANSWER 7.15

DECAY	CIGAR	ISSUE
LODGE	HANDY	CHILD

ANSWER 7.16

6	4	7	9	2	5	1	3	8
5	1	9	3	4	8	2	7	6
3	2	8	7	1	6	4	5	9
7	6	2	1	9	4	3	8	5
9	5	3	8	7	2	6	1	4
4	8	1	6	5	3	9	2	7
8	9	5	2	6	1	7	4	3
2	3	6	4	8	7	5	9	1
1	7	4	5	3	9	8	6	2

ANSWER 7.17

4	6	7	2	3	8	1	9	5
8	2	9	7	5	1	3	6	4
3	5	1	9	4	6	2	8	7
1	4	3	6	8	7	5	2	9
2	7	6	5	1	9	4	3	8
5	9	8	3	2	4	6	7	1
9	3	2	4	7	5	8	1	6
7	8	5	1	6	3	9	4	2
6	1	4	8	9	2	7	5	3

ANSWER 8.02

M	O	C			T	A	M	S		W	H	A
H	I	E	S		W	R	A	P		H	A	S
O	L	L	A		O	S	S	A		I	R	K
			T	A	S			C	O	T	E	S
T	R	I	E	R		S	H	E	D			
A	A	S		F	L	O	E		S	A	C	S
N	I	L		S	A	L	E	S		I	L	K
S	L	E	D		C	O	L	A		D	U	I
		U	S	E	S		G	R	E	E	T	
C	A	D	E	T		G	O	A				
O	V	A		O	G	R	E		P	A	V	E
C	O	W		W	H	E	E		S	A	I	L
A	W	N		S	I	B	S		H	A	M	

ANSWER 8.03

In real love you want the other person's good. In romantic love you want the other person.

—Margaret Anderson

ANSWER 8.04

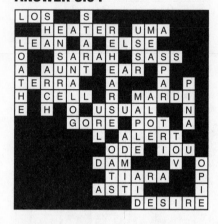

ANSWER 8.05

7	4	5	8	3	1	6	9	2
1	6	3	4	2	9	7	5	8
2	9	8	5	7	6	1	3	4
8	3	7	2	6	5	9	4	1
4	1	6	7	9	3	8	2	5
5	2	9	1	8	4	3	7	6
3	5	2	9	1	8	4	6	7
6	7	1	3	4	2	5	8	9
9	8	4	6	5	7	2	1	3

ANSWER 8.06

```
2 8 3 4 1 7 9 5 6
1 6 5 3 9 8 4 7 2
4 7 9 5 6 2 8 1 3
5 2 7 9 8 4 6 3 1
6 1 4 7 3 5 2 9 8
9 3 8 6 2 1 7 4 5
8 5 2 1 4 9 3 6 7
7 4 6 2 5 3 1 8 9
3 9 1 8 7 6 5 2 4
```

ANSWER 8.07

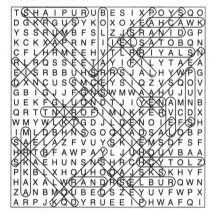

ANSWER 8.08

START	NIECE	UNCUT
RIFLE	ERROR	NURSE

ANSWER 8.09

```
A L T S ■ A R K ■ M O T H
R O O T ■ P E A ■ A L O E
T O T E ■ S T Y ■ S E L L
■ ■ L E E ■ ■ S O U P
C A M E L ■ C A S E ■ ■
O R A ■ A F O R E ■ A R B
K I T ■ P L O T S ■ R I A
E A T ■ S A L S A ■ C O N
■ ■ T E T S ■ M A S T S
A C M E ■ ■ S E R ■ ■
L O A N ■ P I E ■ R A T S
P A N S ■ A R E ■ A L A E
S T Y E ■ D E S ■ S E R A
```

ANSWER 8.10

Many who seem to be struggling with adversity are happy; many, amid great affluence, are utterly miserable.

　　　　—Tacitus

ANSWER 8.11

Surely what a man does when he is caught off his guard is the best evidence as to what sort of man he is.

　　　　—C. S. Lewis

ANSWER 8.12

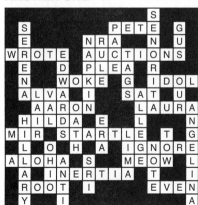

ANSWER 8.13

```
7 1 2 9 3 4 8 5 6
5 8 6 1 7 2 9 4 3
9 4 3 6 5 8 2 7 1
1 6 5 2 8 9 4 3 7
3 9 7 4 1 5 6 2 8
4 2 8 3 6 7 5 1 9
6 5 1 8 4 3 7 9 2
8 7 9 5 2 1 3 6 4
2 3 4 7 9 6 1 8 5
```

ANSWER 8.14

THIEF	EXIST	HELLO
ELECT	MINOR	THEME

ANSWER 8.15

HABIT	FANCY	LABOR
EAGLE	STEAM	SHELF

ANSWER 8.16

```
5 8 4 2 9 3 7 6 1
1 3 6 8 4 7 2 5 9
9 2 7 1 6 5 3 8 4
8 9 3 7 2 4 6 1 5
4 7 5 9 1 6 8 2 3
6 1 2 5 3 8 4 9 7
7 6 8 4 5 1 9 3 2
3 5 9 6 7 2 1 4 8
2 4 1 3 8 9 5 7 6
```

ANSWER 8.17

```
7 5 4 9 6 1 3 2 8
9 8 6 2 5 3 4 1 7
1 2 3 4 8 7 5 9 6
3 6 7 1 2 9 8 4 5
4 9 2 5 7 8 1 6 3
5 1 8 6 3 4 2 7 9
2 7 5 8 4 6 9 3 1
6 4 9 3 1 5 7 8 2
8 3 1 7 9 2 6 5 4
```

ANSWER 9.02

```
PSST . AMPS . ORT
ALEE . ROUT . NAE
TORE . SATE . ERN
SEEDS . . . ESSES
. . ARMADA .
GAT . TOIL . STAB
EYES . ANT . SOLO
NENE . SCAT . MAY
. . ASTERS .
BLAST . . . KAPPA
RAP . APES . SLOG
AVE . BARE . PELE
DAD . SPAT . SALE
```

ANSWER 9.03

Be glad of life because it gives you the chance to love, to work, to play, and to look up at the stars.

— Henry Van Dyke

ANSWER 9.04

ANSWER 9.05

```
5 9 6 2 1 7 3 8 4
2 3 8 4 6 9 5 7 1
1 7 4 8 5 3 2 9 6
4 6 7 5 3 1 9 2 8
3 5 2 9 8 6 1 4 7
8 1 9 7 2 4 6 5 3
6 8 5 3 7 2 4 1 9
9 2 1 6 4 8 7 3 5
7 4 3 1 9 5 8 6 2
```

ANSWER 9.06

```
2 1 6 8 7 3 9 4 5
9 4 7 1 5 2 6 3 8
5 8 3 4 6 9 7 2 1
7 9 1 5 3 8 2 6 4
6 2 8 7 1 4 3 5 9
4 3 5 2 9 6 8 1 7
3 7 4 9 2 5 1 8 6
1 5 2 6 8 7 4 9 3
8 6 9 3 4 1 5 7 2
```

ANSWER 9.07

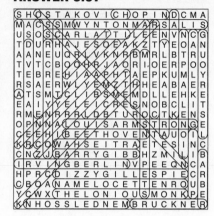

ANSWER 9.08

HATCH	REIGN	SAUCE
USUAL	BAGEL	BRUSH

ANSWER 9.09

```
OWED . MAD . CARD
TOPE . ORE . AGIO
TEEN . BRA . MAGS
OSES . . ELSE .
. . ERGS . TRESS
ODS . OAT . RAVEN
ARENAS . PESETA
RAGES . TOE . SAG
STOAT . HITS .
. TSAR . THAT
TYNE . MOP . AERO
AEON . ANA . TRIM
TARS . HES . SODS
```

ANSWER 9.10

The man who does not read good books has no advantage over the man who cannot read them.

— Mark Twain

ANSWER 9.11

Remember happiness doesn't depend upon who you are or what you have; it depends solely on what you think.
—Dale Carnegie

ANSWER 9.12

A					P		P	I	T		S
M	A	M	E	T		I	P	A	S	S		H	O	P
O			I		O	A	T	E	S			A		E
R		I	S	L	E	T	S		A	T	T	I	R	E
E			A	T	L	A	S		L		A			D
			W		B		E			S	W	A	Y
A	U	G			A	B	S	E	N	T			L
L				E			Y	A	N	K	S
O			V	A	L	U	E	R			A
U	F	O		H	E	M	S		T	O	O	L		U
L			R		A			T	R	E	Y	S
S	A	L	E		S	G	T		L		I	S	E	E
X			H	E	N		M	I	L	O			A
E			E		A			T	E	N	O	R
N	A	R	R	O	W				E			S

ANSWER 9.13

6	2	8	4	1	9	5	7	3
4	1	5	6	7	3	2	9	8
3	7	9	5	2	8	4	1	6
5	4	7	9	3	6	8	2	1
9	8	1	2	4	7	6	3	5
2	6	3	1	8	5	7	4	9
7	9	6	3	5	2	1	8	4
1	3	2	8	6	4	9	5	7
8	5	4	7	9	1	3	6	2

ANSWER 9.14

AWFUL	TENSE	EGYPT
MARSH	LATER	METAL

ANSWER 9.15

MEDAL	ALONG	FRONT
LEGAL	EQUAL	FLAME

ANSWER 9.16

4	5	7	1	9	6	8	3	2
1	8	2	7	3	5	9	6	4
9	6	3	8	4	2	1	7	5
5	7	1	4	8	9	3	2	6
3	2	8	6	1	7	5	4	9
6	9	4	2	5	3	7	8	1
2	1	9	3	6	8	4	5	7
7	3	5	9	2	4	6	1	8
8	4	6	5	7	1	2	9	3

ANSWER 9.17

3	9	6	2	1	7	5	4	8
7	4	5	6	8	3	1	9	2
2	8	1	4	9	5	6	7	3
5	2	7	8	3	9	4	1	6
9	6	4	1	7	2	8	3	5
8	1	3	5	6	4	7	2	9
6	3	9	7	5	1	2	8	4
4	7	8	9	2	6	3	5	1
1	5	2	3	4	8	9	6	7

ANSWER 10.02

L	A	B			B	R	A	G		M	A	T
A	G	A	R		R	O	T	E		A	G	E
S	O	M	A		O	D	E	S		N	U	N
			T	A	S			T	R	E	E	D
S	A	V	E	R		G	L	E	E
O	B	I		B	R	A	E		S	O	T	S
A	L	S		S	A	T	E	S		A	H	A
K	E	E	L		C	O	R	E		S	E	N
		A	P	E	R		M	A	T	E	S
S	L	A	T	S		M	I	L
E	O	N		A	C	H	E		B	R	A	S
A	C	T		L	O	O	T		S	A	S	H
L	I	E		M	O	P	E		S	P	Y

ANSWER 10.03

You don't get to choose how you're going to die. Or when. You can only decide how you're going to live. Now.
—Joan Baez

ANSWER 10.04

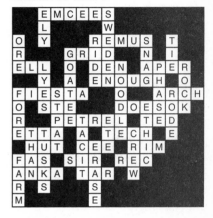

ANSWER 10.05

3	7	4	9	8	1	2	6	5
6	1	5	7	2	4	9	3	8
9	2	8	3	6	5	4	1	7
1	3	2	8	4	9	7	5	6
4	5	9	6	1	7	8	2	3
7	8	6	5	3	2	1	9	4
8	4	3	2	9	6	5	7	1
5	9	1	4	7	3	6	8	2
2	6	7	1	5	8	3	4	9

ANSWER 10.06

8	4	5	2	1	3	9	7	6
9	3	7	6	4	5	8	2	1
6	2	1	7	8	9	5	3	4
2	7	6	8	9	4	3	1	5
5	9	8	1	3	2	6	4	7
3	1	4	5	7	6	2	9	8
1	5	9	4	2	8	7	6	3
4	6	3	9	5	7	1	8	2
7	8	2	3	6	1	4	5	9

ANSWER 10.07

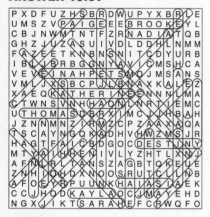

ANSWER 10.08

ERASE	LEASE	LEVER
MAYOR	SOUND	SMELL

ANSWER 10.09

T	A	E		T	H	E	M		S	L	A	M
A	L	L		A	U	R	A		L	A	N	E
P	A	L		S	H	A	D		A	G	E	D
A	S	S	E	S		S	E	A	T			
			L	E	T		B	E	S	T	S	
S	C	A	D		R	O	S	E		H	A	Y
H	O	N		P	I	C	O	T		M	E	N
E	R	S		R	O	A	N		T	O	L	E
S	N	A	R	E		S	P	A				
		E	P	O	S		A	N	G	S	T	
B	O	W	S		L	A	I	N		O	H	O
A	L	I	T		D	I	C	E		B	O	O
Y	E	N	S		S	L	E	D		S	O	N

ANSWER 10.10

The little unremembered acts of kindness and love are the best parts of a person's life.

—William Wordsworth

ANSWER 10.11

One deceit needs many others, and so the whole house is built in the air and must soon come to the ground.

—Baltasar Gracian

ANSWER 10.12

ANSWER 10.13

6	5	9	2	3	1	7	4	8
7	8	2	4	9	6	1	3	5
4	1	3	5	8	7	6	2	9
5	9	7	8	6	2	4	1	3
8	3	6	1	4	5	2	9	7
2	4	1	3	7	9	5	8	6
1	7	8	6	2	3	9	5	4
9	2	4	7	5	8	3	6	1
3	6	5	9	1	4	8	7	2

ANSWER 10.14

EJECT	LEDGE	LATCH
OWNER	CARVE	**CELLO**

ANSWER 10.15

TEETH	ACORN	EXTRA
FAVOR	STORY	**FEAST**

ANSWER 10.16

9	7	1	2	6	8	3	4	5
4	8	2	5	3	1	7	6	9
5	3	6	7	4	9	2	8	1
3	1	9	4	7	5	6	2	8
8	6	4	1	9	2	5	7	3
7	2	5	6	8	3	1	9	4
2	9	8	3	5	6	4	1	7
6	5	7	8	1	4	9	3	2
1	4	3	9	2	7	8	5	6

ANSWER 10.17

3	2	5	7	4	1	8	6	9
1	9	7	2	8	6	3	4	5
8	4	6	9	3	5	7	2	1
2	5	1	8	6	7	9	3	4
6	7	8	4	9	3	1	5	2
9	3	4	5	1	2	6	7	8
7	8	9	6	2	4	5	1	3
5	1	2	3	7	9	4	8	6
4	6	3	1	5	8	2	9	7

ANSWER 11.02

```
OPS  CELL  SIRE
PEE  AREA  TOOL
TEE  SEAM  ANTS
  PROA    PAR
    PSIS   STARS
LASE  OPTS  SEE
OLES  TAO  TENT
AMP  BARN  OATS
MATTE  SEAR
   EEL   LAPS
TWAS  ABRI  HAE
HEAT  SOON  ARM
ETHS  SABE  TIS
```

ANSWER 11.03

Life would be infinitely happier if we could only be born at the age of eighty and gradually approach eighteen.

— Mark Twain

ANSWER 11.04

```
LERNER   WHY
A        A      S
UNLOCK   SHOT   EGG
G   F  NAPA  R   E   R
HALF   O   SPEND   O
  B  OIL   T   B   C
MOON  L   E   LIE   E
  A     SPONGE   R
TRIED   P   A   S
ADD   EASE   RHETT
S  S  CORNEA   IDA
K   COLA   GAIN
S  FADES   FENDER
  PETER   YODEL
D     S     V
```

ANSWER 11.05

8	5	3	9	7	4	6	2	1
1	2	9	5	3	6	4	8	7
4	7	6	8	2	1	5	9	3
2	8	4	1	6	9	3	7	5
6	9	5	7	8	3	2	1	4
7	3	1	4	5	2	9	6	8
9	1	8	2	4	5	7	3	6
5	6	2	3	1	7	8	4	9
3	4	7	6	9	8	1	5	2

ANSWER 11.06

4	2	5	7	1	9	6	8	3
6	8	1	5	3	4	9	2	7
9	3	7	8	2	6	4	5	1
1	7	8	6	9	3	2	4	5
5	6	3	2	4	7	1	9	8
2	4	9	1	8	5	7	3	6
3	5	2	4	7	1	8	6	9
8	1	6	9	5	2	3	7	4
7	9	4	3	6	8	5	1	2

ANSWER 11.07

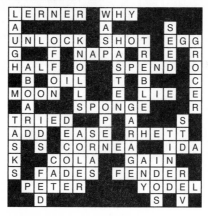

ANSWER 11.08

KNOCK	KNIFE	IRISH
SCRUB	OBESE	KIOSK

ANSWER 11.09

```
DAB  SLOT  MANO
OWE  TUBE  ALAR
REGAINED  SAVE
   CLAY  TONES
AWARE  ELAN
GAME  TROP  SIT
ENISLE  PSEUDO
RED  ORLE  CREW
   SONE  CRESS
SPATS  THRU
CAKE  RHEOSTAT
UNIT  EARN  AMI
PENS  FLEE  MAN
```

ANSWER 11.10

Never worry about the size of your Christmas tree. In the eyes of children, they are all thirty feet tall.

— Larry Wilde

ANSWER 11.11

The highest use of capital is not to make more money, but to make money do more for the betterment of life.

—Henry Ford

ANSWER 11.12

```
A D L I B   P U N   L E A R N
R     O     N   A     R     O
O   O G L E   D Y E S   O   S
D O N U T       H O E     O E
P       S T P     B R A N
S A T   S E C R E T
A     A L A N   D   L     T
T     P O R T   S E E S A W
R O D E O     A   M     L A V
I   U   S O D I U M     L
U N C L E     N   Y O K E   A
M     T     A N N S     G   C
  S T A I R S     A G E N T O
          T                 O
  D O N K E Y       S E A V E R
```

ANSWER 11.13

8	3	9	4	2	1	7	5	6
6	2	7	5	8	3	4	1	9
1	5	4	7	6	9	8	2	3
5	4	1	3	9	7	2	6	8
2	9	3	8	5	6	1	4	7
7	8	6	1	4	2	9	3	5
9	6	8	2	3	4	5	7	1
3	1	2	9	7	5	6	8	4
4	7	5	6	1	8	3	9	2

ANSWER 11.14

LASER	WEDGE	HARDY
ABOUT	ENTER	**WHALE**

ANSWER 11.15

MODEL	YIELD	EARLY
ROBOT	ROAST	**MERRY**

ANSWER 11.16

6	4	2	8	1	9	7	3	5
7	5	1	3	6	2	8	4	9
9	3	8	5	4	7	6	1	2
8	6	9	7	3	5	1	2	4
5	2	4	1	9	8	3	7	6
3	1	7	4	2	6	9	5	8
1	7	5	9	8	4	2	6	3
2	8	3	6	5	1	4	9	7
4	9	6	2	7	3	5	8	1

ANSWER 11.17

6	9	5	3	1	8	7	4	2
4	7	8	2	6	9	5	3	1
1	3	2	7	5	4	8	6	9
2	4	7	9	8	1	6	5	3
8	1	6	5	4	3	2	9	7
3	5	9	6	2	7	1	8	4
5	6	4	1	9	2	3	7	8
9	2	3	8	7	5	4	1	6
7	8	1	4	3	6	9	2	5

ANSWER 12.02

```
S L A T   W A G   S L A W
T A R E   E Y E   P A P A
A C E S   B E N   A W E D
R E S T     S E T T
      Y E S   R E A P S
A R C   M O C H A   R A H
W O O   B R O O D   F R O
L U V   R E S E E   S A W
S E E P Y     S R I
      O O P S   M O R T
T O D S   F I B   A M I E
H O O T   F L U   M I L S
O H M S   T O Y   S T E T
```

ANSWER 12.03

Security is when everything is settled. When nothing can happen to you. Security is the denial of life.

—Germaine Greer

ANSWER 12.04

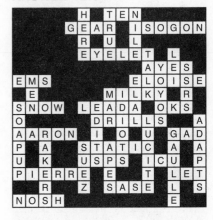

ANSWER 12.05

3	1	6	7	4	8	5	2	9
8	4	9	5	2	3	6	7	1
2	5	7	6	1	9	3	4	8
5	8	2	3	9	1	7	6	4
1	7	4	2	6	5	9	8	3
9	6	3	4	8	7	1	5	2
7	3	8	1	5	4	2	9	6
6	9	1	8	7	2	4	3	5
4	2	5	9	3	6	8	1	7

ANSWER 12.06

```
1 7 8 3 2 4 5 9 6
4 5 9 8 6 1 7 3 2
2 6 3 7 5 9 1 8 4
7 9 1 4 8 2 3 6 5
3 4 6 9 1 5 8 2 7
8 2 5 6 3 7 4 1 9
5 8 7 1 9 6 2 4 3
6 3 2 5 4 8 9 7 1
9 1 4 2 7 3 6 5 8
```

ANSWER 12.07

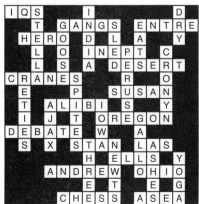

ANSWER 12.08

LEAVE	VERSE	ELOPE
IRONY	DIRTY	DEVIL

ANSWER 12.09

```
C A P   P E P S   S H A G
H I E   A L S O   H O B O
I D S   S K I P   R E A D
S E T A E     S H E
    L O S S   A D A P T
B Y T E   T O G S   F O E
R U E S   O A R   M A L E
I L L   S A K E   I R E S
T E E T H   S W A T
    A A S   R E C A P
A L L S   E A V E   O V A
N E A T   I L I A   N O T
D I M E   S P A S   E W E
```

ANSWER 12.10

In order to succeed, your desire for success should be greater than your fear of failure.

—Bill Cosby

ANSWER 12.11

There is not enough darkness in all the world to put out the light of even one small candle.

—Robert Alden

ANSWER 12.12

ANSWER 12.13

```
8 9 4 1 3 7 5 2 6
2 5 7 9 4 6 3 1 8
1 6 3 5 2 8 7 9 4
5 2 1 8 7 4 6 3 9
3 8 9 6 1 5 2 4 7
7 4 6 2 9 3 8 5 1
9 1 5 7 6 2 4 8 3
4 7 8 3 5 1 9 6 2
6 3 2 4 8 9 1 7 5
```

ANSWER 12.14

ALONE	BEGIN	GOOSE
EQUIP	DOLLY	BADGE

ANSWER 12.15

SEIZE	SCENT	APRON
BURST	RANGE	BRASS

ANSWER 12.16

```
9 1 3 8 6 4 5 7 2
7 5 8 3 2 9 6 1 4
2 6 4 5 1 7 3 8 9
4 3 5 7 8 2 1 9 6
8 7 9 1 5 6 4 2 3
6 2 1 9 4 3 8 5 7
5 4 2 6 7 8 9 3 1
1 9 7 4 3 5 2 6 8
3 8 6 2 9 1 7 4 5
```

ANSWER 12.17

8	1	6	5	7	4	9	3	2
2	3	4	8	1	9	7	6	5
7	9	5	6	3	2	1	4	8
5	6	7	2	4	1	8	9	3
3	4	1	9	8	6	2	5	7
9	2	8	7	5	3	6	1	4
1	7	9	3	2	5	4	8	6
6	8	3	4	9	7	5	2	1
4	5	2	1	6	8	3	7	9

ANSWER 13.02

A crossword grid with the following entries:

FOIL · PLAT · OHM
ANNA · ROPE · BAA
SENT · OUTS · ORS
HAST · TREES
BASED · SAE
AWL · DADA · PASS
KOI · SCOLD · RHO
ELMS · RETE · CUM
OSE · ALONE
SLASH · BANE
LOP · AGON · FRAT
ACE · MORE · TUNA
PAX · STEW · SNIP

ANSWER 13.03

Coming together is a beginning. Keeping together is progress. Working together is success.

—Henry Ford

ANSWER 13.04

A crossword grid with the following entries:

INLOVE · LOOP · FBI
GO · O · E · I · U
E · SPARTA · A · EERIE
T · E · S · S · A
P · SACHET · RUTS
IN · TELL · HEAT · E
N · ONION · O · YARD
UCLA · U · UHOH
POET · DRUG · N
ADE · S · HESSE
PESO · E · M · L
IT · ONCE · AUDIO
N · ID · HEIR · T
ELNINO · LIKES
IN · LASS

ANSWER 13.05

5	3	1	2	6	4	8	7	9
7	9	4	3	8	5	6	2	1
8	6	2	9	1	7	5	3	4
1	8	7	5	2	9	4	6	3
3	4	9	1	7	6	2	5	8
6	2	5	4	3	8	9	1	7
4	1	3	6	9	2	7	8	5
9	7	6	8	5	3	1	4	2
2	5	8	7	4	1	3	9	6

ANSWER 13.06

8	2	5	7	9	4	3	1	6
6	1	3	5	8	2	9	4	7
9	4	7	1	3	6	8	5	2
5	3	2	4	6	8	1	7	9
7	9	4	3	1	5	2	6	8
1	6	8	9	2	7	5	3	4
3	7	1	8	4	9	6	2	5
2	5	9	6	7	1	4	8	3
4	8	6	2	5	3	7	9	1

ANSWER 13.07

ANSWER 13.08

OCEAN   FIGHT   CANAL

SMILE   UNTIL   FOCUS

ANSWER 13.09

A crossword grid with the following entries:

FAR · AMEN · MELD
ODE · VANE · OYER
BOS · ERST · DRAY
TORSI · TEENS
SLAMS · LEAS
CITE · PERT · TAB
AMERCE · REDONE
BAD · LAWS · ROTA
SOLI · SOLAR
ARCED · SLAPS
LILT · PEAS · HAH
FEAT · ISMS · EVE
ALMS · STAY · DAP

ANSWER 13.10

I don't want any yes-men around me. I want everybody to tell me the truth even if it costs them their jobs.

—Samuel Goldwyn

ANSWER 13.11

We all live with the objective of being happy; our lives are all different and yet the same.

—Anne Frank

ANSWER 13.12

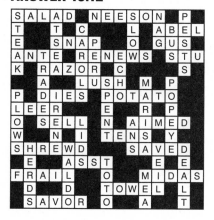

ANSWER 13.13

2	9	3	6	1	4	8	5	7
6	5	4	8	7	3	2	9	1
1	7	8	2	5	9	6	3	4
4	6	7	5	2	1	9	8	3
9	2	1	3	6	8	7	4	5
3	8	5	9	4	7	1	2	6
7	3	6	4	9	2	5	1	8
5	4	2	1	8	6	3	7	9
8	1	9	7	3	5	4	6	2

ANSWER 13.14

NASAL	BEARD	ALLOW
OUNCE	CHAIR	BACON

ANSWER 13.15

CAMEL	AGAIN	SLEEP
RAZOR	FAIRY	SCARF

ANSWER 13.16

4	6	1	7	3	2	5	8	9
5	3	2	8	9	4	7	6	1
8	9	7	5	1	6	4	2	3
1	2	9	4	8	3	6	7	5
6	7	8	9	2	5	3	1	4
3	5	4	6	7	1	8	9	2
2	1	5	3	6	7	9	4	8
9	4	6	2	5	8	1	3	7
7	8	3	1	4	9	2	5	6

ANSWER 13.17

1	5	7	3	8	2	9	4	6
8	9	6	4	5	1	7	2	3
2	4	3	6	7	9	1	8	5
5	2	9	1	3	8	4	6	7
7	3	1	2	4	6	8	5	9
4	6	8	7	9	5	2	3	1
3	8	5	9	1	4	6	7	2
9	7	2	8	6	3	5	1	4
6	1	4	5	2	7	3	9	8

ANSWER 14.02

H	M	M		B	E	S	T		B	A	T	E
E	A	U		A	M	A	S		A	L	E	F
H	I	T		S	U	L	K		S	T	A	T
	D	E	L	E			S	O	T			
		A	R	M	S		R	E	M	A	P	
A	B	E	D		A	L	B	A		A	X	E
W	I	G		O	R	E	A	D		M	O	N
E	K	E		R	E	E	S		S	A	N	D
S	E	R	A	C		P	E	S	O			
		N	A	N			T	U	B	S		
B	R	A	T		A	S	H	Y		L	A	C
R	O	L	E		M	O	U	E		O	K	A
R	E	B	S		E	W	E	S		B	I	D

ANSWER 14.03

And in the end, it's not the years in your life that count. It's the life in your years.

—Abraham Lincoln

ANSWER 14.04

O	V	E	N	S			L							
L					K	A	P	O	K					
I	V	I	I				G		I		W			
E		D		P			C	H	I	C			G	
R	O	L	L	E	R		S		A	T	O	R	A	
		E		D	E	P	T	H	S		B	E	R	T
	H		L	A	H		U	M	P	I	R	E		E
S	E	X		L	I	M	B	O		T	A	L	E	S
	B		R		R		S	I	R	S		M		
O	R	C	A		E	R	N		Y		C	A	R	
E		K		O					I		I			
W	E	E	V	I	L			O	R	A	L	S		
				E	L	A	I	N	E			O		
O	G	R	E	S	S			E		W	O	W		

ANSWER 14.05

1	5	2	6	4	3	7	9	8
3	7	4	9	8	1	5	6	2
9	6	8	2	7	5	3	1	4
8	9	7	5	1	2	6	4	3
4	3	1	8	9	6	2	7	5
6	2	5	7	3	4	9	8	1
5	8	3	1	6	9	4	2	7
7	4	6	3	2	8	1	5	9
2	1	9	4	5	7	8	3	6

ANSWER 14.06

1	8	7	4	3	9	6	2	5
3	5	2	7	8	6	9	1	4
9	4	6	5	2	1	8	3	7
6	1	8	3	5	2	7	4	9
7	3	9	1	6	4	2	5	8
4	2	5	9	7	8	1	6	3
2	9	3	8	1	5	4	7	6
5	6	4	2	9	7	3	8	1
8	7	1	6	4	3	5	9	2

ANSWER 14.07

ANSWER 14.08

DELAY	YOUNG	IDEAL
ROBIN	ANGER	**DAIRY**

ANSWER 14.09

```
T W O   P I E D   A N I L
R I D   A C T A   C O D E
A D D   S H A Y   T E L S
M E S A S       A S S E T
    S E A M E N
P O R K   T O G A   P O P
O X Y   O R L E S   R U E
W O E   R I D S   P O R N
    C A S T L E
S C A B S     O R C A S
P A L E   P L U S   O R C
U R G E   H I R E   P I A
D E A R   I N N S   E L M
```

ANSWER 14.10

The world we have created is a product of our thinking; it cannot be changed without changing our thinking.

—Albert Einstein

ANSWER 14.11

Whatever is at the center of our life will be the source of our security, guidance, wisdom, and power.

—Stephen Covey

ANSWER 14.12

```
          S A N T A
S E A S O N   N   L A V A
I     E   A F T   A     X
S W A N   I   S K I M   W E B
I     S T L O     O E R     I
O       R U B Y     E     D
  A U R O R A   R   A R A B S
  R     H   T W O       T
  I   C A P E   N     S H O P
  A   R   D E C A D E     R
S A R A     S   I   L I M O
  R   O A K   S   D     S
H A M   N   I G L O O   E
A   B L O O M   E   M I N
Y O U     O
```

ANSWER 14.13

9	8	7	2	4	1	6	5	3
2	6	1	9	3	5	7	4	8
4	3	5	7	8	6	2	1	9
7	5	2	3	6	4	9	8	1
6	1	8	5	2	9	3	7	4
3	9	4	8	1	7	5	6	2
1	4	3	6	5	2	8	9	7
8	7	6	4	9	3	1	2	5
5	2	9	1	7	8	4	3	6

ANSWER 14.14

STEEL	DISCO	AMUSE
AGREE	LEMON	**SALAD**

ANSWER 14.15

SHEEP	ELBOW	AFTER
JUICE	NANNY	**JEANS**

ANSWER 14.16

3	7	6	8	2	5	4	1	9
4	8	1	7	3	9	5	6	2
2	5	9	1	6	4	8	7	3
8	9	5	4	1	2	6	3	7
6	2	4	9	7	3	1	5	8
7	1	3	6	5	8	9	2	4
1	4	7	2	8	6	3	9	5
9	3	2	5	4	1	7	8	6
5	6	8	3	9	7	2	4	1

ANSWER 14.17

```
2 3 1 4 9 8 5 7 6
8 4 5 2 7 6 1 9 3
9 6 7 5 1 3 4 2 8
5 7 2 9 6 4 3 8 1
6 1 4 3 8 7 9 5 2
3 8 9 1 5 2 6 4 7
4 5 8 7 3 1 2 6 9
1 2 6 8 4 9 7 3 5
7 9 3 6 2 5 8 1 4
```

ANSWER 15.02

```
R U S E   B E G S   C H I
U S E S   A G H A   Y A R
T E X T   L O I N   S K I
      E L L       T A T E S
M A D R E   I D O L
I V Y   D O O R   T O Y S
L E N T   G N U   O R A L
T R E E   L I M B   T W A
    A L E C   R A S P Y
S A B R A   S O L
C U E   M Y N A   P H E W
U T A   B O I L   H E A R
M O M   S U P S   A W R Y
```

ANSWER 15.03

Always leave something to wish for;
otherwise you will be miserable from
your very happiness.

—Baltasar Gracian

ANSWER 15.04

```
          P                 T     E
      N I P           C R A W L
  D E E R     A       O     S   F
  O     S A M B A     A   I   T
S C O T T     E D E N     E D S
  S     E A T E R       L     T
        B       P A R I S     E
        B A T S     N O V E L
  C     F O X     E K E S     R
F L A     T I E S O N     U S O
  A     K I S S     R         A
  W H I R     A X E S     D   R
        T O P         A C L U
        E N O C H     A   D A M
A I L S E     E       A T T Y S
```

ANSWER 15.05

```
9 3 1 7 4 2 5 8 6
5 8 4 9 3 6 2 1 7
7 6 2 1 8 5 3 9 4
8 1 9 6 7 3 4 2 5
3 4 5 8 2 1 7 6 9
2 7 6 4 5 9 8 3 1
1 5 3 2 9 7 6 4 8
6 2 8 5 1 4 9 7 3
4 9 7 3 6 8 1 5 2
```

ANSWER 15.06

```
4 8 3 7 6 9 1 2 5
5 1 6 2 4 3 8 7 9
9 7 2 5 8 1 6 4 3
2 6 1 8 5 7 9 3 4
3 4 7 1 9 6 2 5 8
8 9 5 3 2 4 7 1 6
7 5 4 6 1 8 3 9 2
1 2 8 9 3 5 4 6 7
6 3 9 4 7 2 5 8 1
```

ANSWER 15.07

```
S T A R F I S H R S H A R K B R T A B P
G U P P Y O Y U S U S N A P P E R S E D
X B K G J A B Y D I B H R L I A P L H
Y I M T U O O S E N F J H A Z L T P T L
T L B L U E G I L L Y D H C M L U R R E
M A R L I N C P T Q L W O G E O B U S
Y H P E R C H O O U L O N O E G R U T S
H L A G T Z U D R C E R W M G N T W E U
B H O N C R B K R M J M E T R A O A O M
K G O O U C B A R R A C U D A N L G E Q
R X D P L T P O L L A C S L X I T U Y Z
J G W S F P A P S S P X X I L U L V A N
O Z R R I U H B C A Z C M E E L O S B Y
A Y H E G F F I S R O A P I R H A L A A
R C K T I F L S N D A M A L O E H L F C
S I B S Y E E I D I O B Z N C Z L O I R
P D U B J R X A K N M C A T F I S H W N
D S T O U K H E Y E L L A W Z V N C V N
T C B L H J H I N R C M N Q B H U O S W
K N F Y S Z X S C L N Z S V K F S G D U
```

ANSWER 15.08

POINT   HAPPY   ATLAS
CHALK   EMPTY   PEACH

ANSWER 15.09

```
O H S   S E C S   A B S
P O U T   L E A P   D I P
E W E R   U L N A   Z O O
      O W E S   C R E S T
S T A T E   D E E
U R B   B A D E   B O S S
N U B   S L U E S   G O A
S E E D   L I D O   R U G
    Y A Y     A P E R S
S P E E D   T A R O
T U G   A D O S   P L A N
E R G   G U N K   S I N E
P R Y   E G G S   B Y E
```

ANSWER 15.10

My goal is simple. It is a complete
understanding of the universe, why it is
as it is and why it exists at all.

—Stephen Hawking

ANSWER 15.11

There are only two tragedies in life: one is not getting what one wants, and the other is getting it.

—Oscar Wilde

ANSWER 15.12

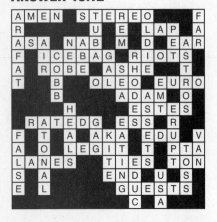

ANSWER 15.16

7	6	2	3	5	9	1	4	8
1	3	9	4	6	8	2	5	7
5	8	4	2	1	7	3	9	6
3	1	7	6	4	2	9	8	5
2	9	6	5	8	1	4	7	3
4	5	8	9	7	3	6	1	2
6	4	1	8	2	5	7	3	9
9	7	5	1	3	6	8	2	4
8	2	3	7	9	4	5	6	1

ANSWER 15.17

4	2	3	1	7	8	6	9	5
8	6	1	3	9	5	7	2	4
5	9	7	4	6	2	1	8	3
6	8	4	5	2	3	9	1	7
7	3	9	8	1	6	4	5	2
1	5	2	7	4	9	8	3	6
2	4	5	6	8	1	3	7	9
3	1	6	9	5	7	2	4	8
9	7	8	2	3	4	5	6	1

ANSWER 15.13

2	8	7	3	9	4	1	6	5
4	6	5	1	2	8	7	9	3
1	9	3	5	6	7	2	4	8
7	2	8	9	5	1	4	3	6
5	1	6	2	4	3	8	7	9
3	4	9	7	8	6	5	1	2
8	7	1	6	3	2	9	5	4
6	5	2	4	1	9	3	8	7
9	3	4	8	7	5	6	2	1

ANSWER 15.14

APPLE   ALIEN   WATER
KNOWN   EIGHT   **AWAKE**

ANSWER 15.15

RELAX   FIRST   OFFER
OASIS   LIGHT   **FLOOR**